Harwood Fundamentals of Pure and Applied Economics

WAGE AND EMPLOYMENT PATTERNS IN LABOR CONTRACTS

FUNDAMENTALS OF PURE AND APPLIED ECONOMICS

MACROECONOMICS
In 3 Volumes

I	Wage and Employment Patterns in Labor Contracts	*Cooper*
II	Macroeconomic Policy, Credibility and Politics	*Persson and Tabellini*
III	Reduced Forms of Rational Expectations Models	*Broze et al.*

WAGE AND EMPLOYMENT PATTERNS IN LABOR CONTRACTS

Microfoundations and Macroeconomic Implications

RUSSELL W COOPER

Routledge
Taylor & Francis Group
LONDON AND NEW YORK

First published in 1987 by
Harwood Academic Publishers GmbH

Reprinted in 2001 by
Routledge

2 Park Square, Milton Park, Abingdon, Oxon OX14 4RN

711 Third Avenue, New York, NY 10017

Routledge is an imprint of the Taylor & Francis Group, an informa business

The publishers have made every effort to contact authors/copyright holders of the works reprinted in *Harwood Fundamentals of Pure & Applied Economics*. This has not been possible in every case, however, and we would welcome correspondence from those individuals/companies we have been unable to trace.

These reprints are taken from original copies of each book. in many cases the condition of these originals is not perfect. the publisher has gone to great lengths to ensure the quality of these reprints, but wishes to point out that certain characteristics of the original copies will, of necessity, be apparent in reprints thereof.

British Library Cataloguing in Publication Data
A CIP catalogue record for this book
is available from the British Library

Wage and Employment Patterns in Labor Contracts
ISBN 0-415-26924-5
Macroeconomics: 3 Volumes
ISBN 0-415-26923-7
Harwood Fundamentals of Pure & Applied Economics
ISBN 0-415-26907-5

Wage and Employment Patterns in Labor Contracts: Microfoundations and Macroeconomic Implications

Russell W. Cooper
University of Iowa, USA

A volume in the Macroeconomic Theory section
edited by
Jean-Michel Grandmont
CEPREMAP, France

harwood academic publishers
chur · london · paris · new york

Harwood Academic Publishers

Post Office Box 197
London WC2E 9PX
England

58, rue Lhomond
75005 Paris
France

Post Office Box 786
Cooper Station
New York, NY 10276
United States of America

Library of Congress Cataloging-in-Publication Data

Cooper, Russell W., 1955–
Wage and employment patterns in labor contracts.

(Fundamentals of pure and applied economics, vol. 19.
Macroeconomic theory section, ISSN 0191-1708)
Bibliography: p.
Includes index.
1. Wages. 2. Employment (Economic theory)
3. Labor contract. I. Title. II. Series: Fundamentals
of pure and applied economics; vol. 19.
HD4909.C57 1987 331.12′5 86-31947
ISBN 3-7186-0378-0

Contents

Introduction to the Series

Drawing on a personal network, an economist can still relatively easily stay well informed in the narrow field in which he works, but to keep up with the development of economics as a whole is a much more formidable challenge. Economists are confronted with difficulties associated with the rapid development of their discipline. There is a risk of "balkanisation" in economics, which may not be favorable to its development.

Fundamentals of Pure and Applied Economics has been created to meet this problem. The discipline of economics has been subdivided into sections (listed inside). These sections include short books, each surveying the state of the art in a given area.

Each book starts with the basic elements and goes as far as the most advanced results. Each should be useful to professors needing material for lectures, to graduate students looking for a global view of a particular subject, to professional economists wishing to keep up with the development of their science, and to researchers seeking convenient information on questions that incidentally appear in their work.

Each book is thus a presentation of the state of the art in a particular field rather than a step-by-step analysis of the development of the literature. Each is a high-level presentation but accessible to anyone with a solid background in economics, whether engaged in business, government, international organizations, teaching, or research in related fields.

Three aspects of *Fundamentals of Pure and Applied Economics* should be emphasized:

—First, the project covers the whole field of economics, not only theoretical or mathematical economics.

—Second, the project is open-ended and the number of books is not predetermined. If new interesting areas appear, they will generate additional books.
—Last, all the books making up each section will later be grouped to constitute one or several volumes of an Encyclopedia of Economics.

The editors of the sections are outstanding economists who have selected as authors for the series some of the finest specialists in the world.

J. Lesourne *H. Sonnenschein*

Wage and Employment Patterns in Labor Contracts: Microfoundations and Macroeconomic Implications

RUSSELL COOPER[1]

The University of Iowa, USA.

1. OVERVIEW

This monograph investigates the behavior of economies in which the trade of labor services occurs through contracts. In contrast to other commodities (such as currencies and many agricultural products), labor is generally not traded in an auction market between anonymous traders.[2] Instead, the employment relationship is relatively long-term and the terms of exchange are specified in a contract between the worker(s) and a firm. While market forces may have influenced the initial matching of workers and firms, it is useful to think of the ex post exchange of labor as being immune to outside market forces in that the levels of employment of wages are not determined directly by current market conditions. Furthermore, these contracts, particularly their wage component, provide insurance and credit which may not otherwise be available to the contractants. Under this interpretation, labor contracts are complex instruments influencing the allocation of labor time and consumption across states of the world and time which may substitute for

[1] I am grateful to Costas Azariadis for introducing me to many of the issues explored here and for comments on this manuscript. Helpful comments and criticism from Jean-Michel Grandmont, Oliver Hart, Charles Kahn, two anonymous reviewers and my colleagues at Iowa are greatly appreciated. All errors and misperceptions are mine alone.

[2] Other examples of trades which fall outside the auction setting include credit relations, insurance purchases and the consumption of many consumer goods in which customers engage in repeated purchases with a single proprietor.

missing markets. This view of the labor exchange process follows the contributions of Baily [8], Gordon [38] and Azariadis [3] and will form the foundation for our analysis.

Contracts are present in a wide range of countries and in most sectors of these economies. While the structure of these contracts may differ, it is clear that the trade of labor services lies outside of the auction setting. What factors determine the form of these contracts? How well do contracting arrangements function as a means of exchanging labor services? Do we obtain additional understanding of labor market and macroeconomic phenomena once we focus on contract-mediated exchanges?

There is a large and ever-growing literature on labor contracts which seeks to answer these questions. The goal of this monograph is to summarize and synthesize the theoretical contributions to labor and macroeconomics of this approach.[3] For the most part, interest in labor contracts began with the quest by macroeconomists for theoretical support for the wage rigidities often assumed in their models. Despite this macro-motivation, the first contributions to this literature by Baily, Gordon and Azariadis were more microeconomic in nature and focused attention on the nature of contracts at the worker-firm level. As a consequence of this microeconomic research strategy, the contracts literature has also contributed to our understanding of certain labor market phenomena, such as seniority rules, and wage profiles, which have little or no apparent significance in macroeconomics.

To reflect these developments, the approach taken in this monograph will be a blend of micro- and macroeconomics. The analysis begins, in the first section, with a discussion of optimal labor contracts in a partial equilibrium setting. These contracts will be completely unrestricted in that all conceivable types of contingencies will be feasible. The discussion highlights the insurance role played by wages in these contracting models and some general properties of employment fluctuations. We also discuss the relation between the predictions of this model and those arising in a complete contingent markets equilibrium.

---

[3] For other surveys of parts of this material see Azariadis [6], Hart [53] and Rosen [82]. The relationship between these surveys will be discussed in the text where appropriate.

The following section departs from an environment of complete contingent contracts and considers the characteristics of labor arrangements when the set of feasible contracts is restricted. This section illustrates the impact of informational asymmetries, enforcement problems and other restrictions on patterns of wages and employment. In doing so, we generate interesting employment distortions, layoffs and related phenomena.

In Section 4, we turn attention to the macroeconomic implications of the contracting approach. We begin with a brief discussion of contracting arrangements across countries. Next we present a series of models which take these contracting features as given and explore their implications for business cycles and the design of macroeconomic policy. We complete this section by extending the basic contracting model to a macroeconomic setting to obtain some predictions about nominal compensation patterns and economy-wide employment fluctuations. Section 5 summarizes our results and discusses the future prospects for this approach.

Before proceeding further, it may prove useful to discuss the general approach of this monograph and its relation to other reviews of this literature. For the most part, this presentation concentrates on contracting models from a theoretical perspective. The discussion of empirical work is included mainly to provide some perspective on the theory. (This limited attention to the data reflects comparative advantage rather than preferences.) The emphasis, then, is in modeling contractual relations in a variety of environments. I have also tried to pay particular attention to techniques which can be applied to a wide range of problems beyond those considered here.

There are other surveys in the literature which cover some of the same material. Azariadis [6] reviews the literature up to, and including, some of the early work on contracting under asymmetric information. Hart [53] begins from there and presents a fairly complete discussion of contracting under asymmetric information. Rosen [82] covers contracting with symmetric and asymmetric information and explores models with and without worksharing. Rosen's survey offers a slightly different perspective on the literature as he stresses the relationship between contracting models and more traditional models of the labor market.

This monograph attempts to provide more of a macroeconomic

perspective and covers some topics which are omitted from these other reviews. Nonetheless, there is a considerable amount of overlap in the models presented in these four reviews. Moreover, all stress one central theme of the contracting literature: wages do not serve to decentralize labor decisions alone but are used as a means of shifting income across contingencies and time as well. As a consequence, wages do not directly reflect the marginal product of labor nor workers' marginal rates of substitution between consumption and leisure.

2. THE BASIC PARADIGM

The basis for contracts

Before starting the actual analysis, we begin with a statement of the types of economies into which we are placing a labor contract. The contracting approach stems from the incompleteness of insurance and/or credit opportunities for workers. As is well-known, if markets were complete, in the sense of Arrow [2] or Debreu [24], all risks will be shared efficiently and the competitive equilibrium will yield Pareto optimal allocations. In such an economy, workers could then obtain insurance against fluctuations in both their wages *and* employment status. While labor contracts might be part of the complex market structure of this economy, they would be redundent in that the insurance elements of a labor contract could be provided by outside insurance companies.

The starting point of the analysis of labor contracts is the assumption that insurance against employment and compensation risk is not available to workers in the marketplace. We term this an assumption since the models employed generally do not explicitly provide a basis for this incompleteness of outside insurance opportunities. The usual story concerns the inability of insurance firms to perfectly monitor the employment status and wages of workers. Hence moral hazard problems may arise and insurance may not be feasible.

If workers, who are presumably risk averse with respect to fluctuations in their incomes, cannot obtain insurance from insurance companies, what other options do they have for stabilizing their income, and hence consumption? Self-insurance from borrowing and lending in capital markets is one obvious way to stabilize consumption even in the absence of explicit insurance markets. Savings, at least early in life, may be insufficient to provide much insurance at all and borrowing opportunities are presumably limited by an individual's inability to borrow against future labor income. Hence, these options are unlikely to provide sufficient self-insurance and are generally excluded from the analysis.

What of firms, or shareholders? Even if capital markets are incomplete, shareholders can diversify some of the idiosyncratic risk associated with the prospects of an individual firm. As a consequence, shareholder, and thus firms, are thought of as being more capable of absorbing risk than their workers. Given the inability of workers to find insurance elsewhere and in light of the firm's ability to costlessly monitor its workers' employment status, these agents are natural partners for the trading of employment and compensation risks. Labor contracts are therefore seen as serving the functions of allocating both risks and labor services.

As stated by Baily [8]:

> A principal function of captial markets is to allow wealthholders to diversify their holdings and so reduce the risk of their total portfolios. Stockholders, through their greater wealth and expertise, are much better able to bear risks than are workers. The difference in ability to bear risk between the two groups immediately suggests an opportunity to trade. In deciding what wage-employment strategy to set, the firm will be willing to reduce workers' risk. By doing so, the firm is offering a joint product, employment plus an insurance or financial intermediation service.

Based on this incomplete nature of markets and workers' general inability to insure themselves, the prototypical contracting model focuses explicit attention on the firm's provision of insurance to workers and excludes any discussion of borrowing by workers. In addition, savings is ruled out as most of the models are static in nature.

The point of the analysis of contracts is then to understand the implications of this joint role of firms on employment and compensation patterns. While labor contracts are viewed as substitutes for missing markets, this does not immediately imply that the resulting allocations will differ from those generated by complete markets.

Before proceeding further, it is helpful to note that there are other rationales for the existence of contracts. One important approach, associated with the work of Becker [11], Williamson [94] and others, views contracting as a means of dealing with incentive problems stemming from the specificity of human capital investments.[4] This approach does not rely on differences in attitudes towards risk. Instead, contracts arise to bind the parties, ex ante, to shares of the benefits stemming from these investments in human capital. Though these affects are certainly important in the labor market, they will not be central to our discussion.

The next part of this section begins our analysis of contracting models. The approach highlights the bilateral nature of contracts and the exclusion of insurance opportunities outside of the firm for workers.

The basic contracting model

To begin, we consider the characteristics of an optimal labor contract between a firm and a pool of N homogeneous workers. After understanding the employment arrangement between these agents, we can then discuss an equilibrium in the labor market and the determination of a firm's workforce.

The firm has available a technology which produces a single output from the labor input. We assume, to start, that output depends on total worker hours so that "hours" and "people" are perfect substitutes in the production process. Hence we can talk about variations in both the level of employment (L) and in average hours per employed worker (h).

Firms have a stochastic technology which depends on total hours given by

$$q = \tilde{s}f(Lh).$$

Here $f(.)$ is strictly increasing and strictly concave. The technology shock, $\tilde{s}$, takes values in the interval $[\underline{s}, \bar{s}]$ and has a cumulative distribution function, $F(s)$. Alternatively, we could view $\tilde{s}$ as the relative price of the firm's output in terms of some numeraire commodity. We assume, for now, that realizations of $\tilde{s}$ are publicly observable.

Firms value profits (π) with a strictly increasing, concave utility function $V(\pi)$. We will often assume that $V(.)$ is linear and hence

[4] See, also, the discussion in Section III of Hart–Holmstrom [54].

view the firm as risk neutral. Profits, for a given realization of s, are

$$\pi(s) \equiv q(s) - w^e(s)h(s)L(s) - w^u(s)(N - L(s)).$$

In this expression, both hours per worker and the level of employment are dependent on $\tilde{s}$. Hence the dependence of q on $\tilde{s}$ reflects both the levels *and* productivity of these inputs. The variable $w^e(s)$ is the hourly wage paid to employed workers in state s. Since we allow employment fluctuations, we also give the firm the option of paying the $N - L(s)$ unemployed workers severance pay of $w^u(s)$ in state s.[5]

Workers are endowed with one unit of leisure time and consume the single consumption good in the economy (c). Preferences are defined over c and hours worked, h, and are given by $U(c, h)$. We assume that $U_c > 0$, $U_h < 0$ and that $U(\cdot)$ is concave. (Here, and throughout the remainder of the monograph, K_x will refer to the first partial derivative of some function $K(.)$ with respect to x. Second partials and cross-partials are defined in an analogous way). For employed workers, consumption in state s is given by $w^e(s)h(s)$. For unemployed workers, consumption in state s is given by $w^u(s)$ which is a transfer from the firm to the workers in the form of privately provided severance pay. We comment later on the role of publicly provided severance payments.

A contract is viewed as an agreement between the firm and its N workers stipulating the number of employed workers ($L(s)$), their hours ($h(s)$), the wage rate for empolyed workers ($w^e(s)$) and the level of severance pay ($w^u(s)$) in *each* state of nature. Since workers are identical, these functions are not individual specific. This contract is agreed upon *prior* to the realization of $\tilde{s}$. We will use the notation δ to describe a contract so that

$$\delta \equiv \{L(s), h(s), w^e(s), w^u(s)\}.$$

The design of this contract will be the object of our analysis.

Before proceeding, it is worthwhile to note the manner in which this contracting specification reflects our earlier assumptions about the incompleteness of markets. In particular, we have assumed that workers' consumption depends solely on compensation so that there are no insurance opportunities available to them outside of this

[5] The next section discusses some restrictions on the provision of severance pay.

contract and no borrowing or lending. The extent to which the structure of capital markets affects the firms will be modeled through the curvature of $V(.)$. Note further, that we have placed no restrictions whatsoever on δ so that this contract *may* reproduce the complete contingent markets solution.

In predicting the form of δ, it is necessary to understand the constraints the contractants face. One of the more important of these constraints relates to the enforceability of the contract. At this stage we assume that a contract can be enforced by a court of law so that ex post deviations from the agreement by either the worker or the firm are met with punishment sufficient enough for us to ignore the enforcement problem for now. We comment on the appropriateness of this assumption later.

We have also assumed that realizations of $\tilde{s}$ are observable to all parties of the contract. Consequently, the terms of the contract depend directly on $\tilde{s}$ without the inclusion of any incentive compatibility constraints. The next section addresses the implications of asymmetric information on the form of δ.

The final constraint is that of voluntary participation. Both the worker and the firm must be no worse off, in expected utility, from transacting under δ than from trading labor services in an alternative form *or* by not trading in this market at all.

The optimal contract, δ^*, can be characterized by the solution to the problem (P1) of maximize

$$E_s V(\pi(s))$$

subject to $E_s\{\rho(s)U(w^e(s)h(s), h(s)) + (1-\rho(s))U(w^u(s), 0)\} \geq \bar{U}$,

$$1 \geq \rho(s) \geq 0,$$

and

$$1 \geq h(s) \geq 0.$$

The objective function is the firm's valuation of the state-dependent profit stream, where $\pi(s)$ is defined above. The first constraint ensures that workers are willing to participate in the contract if they can obtain a utility level of $\bar{U}$ in another activity. We use the variable $\rho(s)$ to denote the probability that an arbitrarily chosen worker is employed in state s: i.e. $\rho(s) \equiv L(s)/N$. Since workers are identical, we have selected a random rationing scheme. Based on this definition of $\rho(s)$, the left-side of the first constraint is simply the worker's expected utility from a contract δ. The second constraint ensures that $\rho(s)$ is a probability and the third bounds $h(s)$.

It is useful to note that the process of maximizing the firm's expected utility subject to an expected utility constraint for the worker is *not* a crucial part of the problem. We could have used expected utility for the worker in the objective function and placed a constraint on the firm's expected utility or we could have used a weighted average of the expected utilities of the contractants. It is critical though that both parties are willing to participate in the contract. The qualitative properties of the optimal contract will generally be independent of the distribution of the gains from the relationship.

The first constraint will be binding in the solution to this programming problem since the firm could otherwise profitably reduce wages, in some state, without losing workers. Using λ as the multiplier on the participation constraint, letting U_c^e and U_c^u denote the marginal utilities of consumption when employed and unemployed, denoting the marginal disutility of work by U_h^e, and ignoring (for now) the constraints on $\rho(s)$ and $h(s)$, the first-order conditions (for all s) are:

$$sf'(hL) = -U_h^e/U_c^e \equiv G(c, h) \tag{1}$$

$$U_c^e = N/\lambda V'(\pi(s)) \tag{2}$$

$$U_c^u = N/\lambda V'(\pi(s)) \tag{3}$$

and

$$shf' = w^e h - w^u - \left(\frac{U^e - U^u}{U_c^e}\right).^{6} \tag{4}$$

In these expressions, the dependence of hours, employment, etc. on $\tilde{s}$ has been suppressed as have some of the arguments of the functions. The first equation ensures equality in the marginal rates of substitution between hours and wages for the firm and a representative worker. If (1) did not hold, then for a given $L(s)$, there would be mutually advantageous adjustments in $h(s)$ and $w^e(s)$ ex post. These will be referred to as "productive efficiency conditions." Equations (2) and (3) are expressions for optimal risk sharing between the agents. These conditions, first analyzed by

[6] We discuss the role of the constraints on $\rho(s)$ and $h(s)$ below.

Borch [14], guarantee that the marginal rate of substitution of income between the parties is equal across states of nature. If these conditions did not hold, it would be possible to find state-dependent transfers between the parties which would increase both of their expected utilities. Putting (2) and (3) together, worker's marginal utility of consumption is equalized across states of employment and unemployment as well. Finally, (4) provides information on the value of adjustments in L. The left-side is the gain to the firm of increasing L in state s for *given* h. The right-side represents the costs of employing the extra worker. The first two terms together represent the net cost of employment. The final term is an adjustment in compensation for the risk to workers associated with altering the employment rule. The magnitude of this risk adjustment (described in more detail below) depends on the differences in worker's utilities between states of employment and unemployment and the workers' attitudes towards risk.

Conditions (1)–(4) make clear a very important theme in the contracting approach. In contrast to the situation of ex post spot markets, wages (or total compensation per worker) do not play a central role in allocating labor resources. This allocation of labor time is undertaken directly in the contract by the independent specification of the $h(s)$ and $L(s)$ schedules. That is, neither $h(s)$ nor $L(s)$ correspond to the demand for hours and workers by a firm taking $w^e(s)$ as given. Wages, instead, play an insurance role as determined by (2)–(3). In some extreme cases, the insurance features of the contract are entirely separate from the allocation of labor services. The consequences of this separation of employment from compensation is a theme we return to frequently in the subsequent discussion.

Interpreting the results of the basic model

As discussed previously, one of the primary motivations for the contracting approach is to understand compensation and employment patterns. In particular, empirical evidence suggests that wages tend to be inflexible relative to employment levels in many economies. The form of employment adjustment, either through variation in average hours or the number of workers, tends to differ across countries and sectors as well.

At least implicitly, conditions (1)–(4) provide all of the information on the determination of these variables. To a large extent, the characteristics of the optimal contract depend on properties of agents' preferences beyond those already assumed. There are some results, however, which emerge from the analysis almost immediately.

Equations (1) and (4) describe the two ways in which the contractants can alter total employment: by changing average hours or by changing the number of workers employed. Since the technology depends only on the product of these two inputs, firm's output is independent of the mixture between h and L. Workers, however, face the risk of layoff if $L < N$ in any state. Even though (3)–(4) indicate that workers receive some severance pay, they are generally *not* indifferent between states of being employed and unemployed (an exception is discussed below). Hence, the parties may agree to eliminate layoff risk entirely by setting $L(s) = N$ for all s.

PROPOSITION 1 *In the solution to P1, $L(s) = N$ for all s.*[7]

Proof. Suppose, to the contrary, that in an optimal contract δ^*, there exists a state $\hat{s}$ with $L(\hat{s}) < N$. Given that $\hat{s}$ occurs, workers' expected utility is given by

$$\rho(\hat{s})U(w^e(\hat{s})h(\hat{s}), h(\hat{s})) + (1 - \rho(\hat{s}))U(w^u(\hat{s}), 0).$$

where $w^e(\hat{s})$, $h(\hat{s})$, $\rho(\hat{s})$ and $w^u(\hat{s})$ are given in δ^*.

Consider an alternative contract $\tilde{\delta}$ which specifies $\tilde{L}(\hat{s}) = N$,

$$\tilde{h}(\hat{s}) = \frac{h(\hat{s})L(\hat{s})}{N},$$

$$\tilde{w}^e(\hat{s}) = \rho(\hat{s})w^e(\hat{s}) + (1 - \rho(\hat{s}))w^u(\hat{s}) \quad \text{and} \quad \tilde{w}^u(\hat{s}) = 0.$$

For states other than $\hat{s}$, $\tilde{\delta}$ is assumed to be identical to δ^*. The firm is indifferent between $\tilde{\delta}$ and δ^* while workers prefer $\tilde{\delta}$ to δ^* given the assumed concavity of $U(c, h)$ and the construction of $\tilde{w}^e(\hat{s})$. Hence a contract with layoffs in any state cannot be a solution to P1. QED.

[7] Recall that P1 is the optimization problem used to generate the optimal contract.

Using Proposition 1, we can now investigate the determination of hours and wages in optimal contracts. To do so, we set $L(s) = N$ for all s and determine hours of work and compensation levels from (1) and (2).

PROPOSITION 2 *In the optimal contract, $h(s)$ is an increasing function of s if firms are sufficiently close to being risk neutral.*

Proof. See Appendix A.

The proof of Proposition 2 in Appendix A proceeds by totally differentiating Eqs (1) and (2) given that $L(s) = N$. As shown by Rosen [82], if the firm is risk neutral and workers are risk averse, employment increases with the state s. This result contrasts with the emphasis on income and substitution effects in the labor supply literature. In an optimal contract between a risk averse worker and a risk neutral firm, income effects are not present due to the risk sharing. As a consequence, employment fluctuations are driven by substitution effects.

When the firm is not risk neutral, the appendix shows that the effect of s on hours can be ambiguous. The slope of the hours schedule depends on the attitudes towards risk by both contractants and the degree to which leisure is a normal good in workers' preferences. As in the traditional labor supply problem, both income and substitution effects are present again. Nonetheless, if firms are close to being risk neutral, hours will always be monotonically increasing in s.

These two propositions provide us with most of the general information concerning movements in employment and hours in an optimal contract. The remainder of this section is devoted to a discussion of the patterns of wages and compensation that may emerge in the optimal contract. We do so by exploring some useful examples.

(*i*) *Risk neutral firms.* As a starting point, assume that shareholders can fully diversify the firm's risk. Further assume that managers' interests coincide with those of shareholders so firms behave as if they were risk neutral.[8] We will continue to assume that workers are risk averse.

[8] Without this assumption, the manager's compensation may reflect the level of profits through the design of an incentive contract between the firm's owners and the manager. If the manager is risk averse and cannot diversify away the profit risk, the firm's decisions may reflect the manager's risk aversion.

With $V''=0$, (2) simplifies to

$$U_c^e = N/\lambda \quad \text{for all } s. \tag{5}$$

Optimal risk sharing now implies that the workers' marginal utility of consumption (equivalently income) is constant across states of the world. Note that (5) does not imply that either the wage rate or total compensation is state independent since U_c^e may depend on hours worked.

To obtain more precise predictions, we can place some additional structure on workers' preferences. These restrictions, combined with firm risk neutrality, help bring to light some important aspects of contracting models.

Assume that $U(c, h) = \hat{U}(c - kh)$ where $\hat{U}$ is strictly increasing and strictly concave. In this specification of preferences, workers' demand for leisure is independent of income. The parameter k represents the worker's disutility of working an extra unit of time. This case of perfect substitutability has been a leading example in the contracts (and incentives) literature.

With these preferences and firm risk neutrality, (2) implies that

$$(w^e - k)h = \hat{U}^{-1}(\bar{U}). \tag{6}$$

That is, optimal insurance implies that the worker's level of utility is constant across states of nature. This constant level of utility is, of course, $\bar{U}$ since the constraints in (P1) must hold.

With these preferences, (1) becomes

$$sf'(hN) = k. \tag{7}$$

So that, by productive efficiency, total hours are set to equalize the marginal product of an extra hour with the worker's (constant) marginal rate of substitution between consumption and labor hours. In some circumstances, (7) cannot be met without violating the constraint that $h \leq 1$ for all workers. When this occurs, all workers are employed full time.

The combination of firm risk neutrality and worker preferences in which consumption and leisure are perfect substitutes represents a leading example in the contracting literature. The implications of insurance are quite clear as is the nature of the employment rule. We return to this case later in our discussion of contracting under asymmetric information.

A second useful case occurs when workers' preferences are

separable: i.e. $U_{ch}(.) \equiv 0$. With this restriction, (5) implies that total compensation is constant across states of nature. As a consequence, wages per hour and averge hours vary inversely. Unless we add an additional assumption about variations in hours (as we do later), the model does not predict constant wage *rates* even though workers have separable preferences and the firm is risk neutral.

As for hours, (1) continues to hold here and ensures an ex post equalization of marginal rates of substitution between the contractants. From this condition and noting that $U_c^e(.)$ is independent of s (from (5) with $U_{ch}^e \equiv 0$), we see immediately that total hours increase with s (as stipulated in Proposition 2).

(*ii*) *Risk neutral workers.* Now we assume that firms are risk averse but that workers are risk neutral. Although this case seems contrary to the previously stated view that labor contracts help to shift risk from workers to firms, the case of worker risk neutrality and firm risk aversion has been useful in understanding the implications of asymmetric information for the design of contracts. This situation may arise if we introduce moral hazard problems within the firm so that risk averse managers face uncertainty in their compensation schemes. Hence, firms may act as though they were risk averse.

Suppose that worker's preferences are represented by $U(c, h) = c - kh$. In this case, the model is similar to the first case explored above except for the reversal in attitudes towards risk by the contractants. With risk neutral workers and risk averse firms, the former insure the latter by stabilizing profits across states of nature. That is, (2) now implies that $\pi(s)$ is constant across states of nature.

Equation (1) implies that total hours are set to equalize the marginal product of labor ($sf'(hN)$) with the marginal disutility of an extra hour, k. Condition (4) simplifies to (1) as in the earlier case. Hence, once again, the contract efficiently determines total hours.

It is useful to contrast this case with the one explored above in which consumption and leisure were perfect substitutes for the risk averse worker. As emphasized earlier, the optimal labor contract disembodies the payment of compensation from the determination of the employment level. Comparing these cases brings this point out quite clearly. The rule for determining total hours is identical in these two cases despite the reversal of the attitudes toward risk. The compensation schedule is set to share this risk efficiently *without* influencing the employment rules.

In general, altering the risk preferences of the two parties will affect both the employment and compensation schedules. Only when consumption and leisure are perfect substitutes (i.e. no income effects) can we completely separate risk sharing from employment.

(*iii*) *Restrictions on hours.* As a final example, we consider restrictions on hours. Many of the leading contracting papers consider economies in which the adjustment of total hours occurs by hiring and firing workers rather than through worksharing. We certainly do observe both layoffs and variations in average hours in the data so it is useful to consider models which focus on layoffs.

To do so, we go to the extreme and assume that all employed workers supply a unit of time. These restrictions on hours can be motivated by non-convexities in workers' preferences or a lack of perfect substitutability between hours and people in the production process. With either of these modifications of the model, Proposition 1 no longer holds.

With $h(s) = 1$ for all employed workers, the optimal contract is characterized by (2)–(4). Equations (2) and (3) are, once again, conditions for efficient risk sharing between the parties.

The interesting part of this formulation of the contracting problem stems from (4). To understand it, we first return to review Proposition 1.

The logic behind Proposition 1 was that employment variations brought about through layoffs were costly to the firm. This cost arose due to risk aversion on the part of workers. Given the assumed concavity of $U(c, h)$, workers preferred to share the total hours and wages available in a given state rather than face a lottery between being employed and unemployed.

When worksharing is no longer feasible, the parties to the contract bear the cost of the risk induced by employment adjustment. The net cost of employing an additional worker (for $h = 1$ hours) is given by

$$(w^e - w^u) - \left(\frac{U^e - U^u}{U_c^e}\right)$$

from (4). The first term is the differential between the employment and unemployment wages. The second term is a risk premium associated with the additional risk created by the employment lottery. The difference between U^e and U^u (which could be negative) indicates the amount of layoff risk workers face. The size of this differential and hence its implications for the employment rule depends on the attitudes toward risk of the workers. (It would also be dependent upon the level of publicly provided unemployment insurance.)

For example, consider once again the special case in which the firm is risk neutral and $U(c, h) = \hat{U}(c - kh)$ where h equals either zero or one. Equations (2) and (3) then imply that

$$w^e - k = w^u$$

so that the worker is indifferent between being employed and unemployed. In this case, (4) (ignoring integer problems) simplifies to

$$sf' = k$$

as we obtained earlier. With consumption and work as perfect substitutes, workers don't mind the employment lottery. While Proposition 1 holds (weakly) for this case, the optimal contract actually does not uniquely determine the split between average hours and the level of employment.

For preferences other than this special case, U^e and U^u will generally diverge. As a consequence, employment risk, even in the presence of unrestricted severance pay, is an important part of a layoff decision.

The interested reader can consider alternative specifications for preferences to further understand (4). Since we will be returning to a version of this restricted model in the discussion of Azariadis [3], we will not dwell further on these special cases.

Summarizing the results of the basic contracting model

With the characterization of the optimal contract from (1)–(4), Propositions 1 and 2 and the special cases in mind, it is appropriate to consider what insights the contracting models have generated. One of the most important aspects of the approach concerns the role of wages. As has been emphasized repeatedly, wages do not serve as signals to elicit supplies of, and demands for, labor. The contracting model specifies an employment rule directly while wages (or better, compensation) serve to allocate risk.

One critical consequence of this reinterpretation of wages concerns empirical work on models of labor supply and labor demand. Rosen [82] discusses these issues as well. For the most part these studies start from the presumption that wages (along with other prices) decentralize the allocation of labor time. Hence, subject to conditions of identification, movements in wages can be used to help estimate parameters of production functions and preferences. To the extent, though, that contracts of the type modeled here are present, this estimation technique can be misleading.

As an example of this point, suppose an econometrician attempted to estimate properties of a production function under a hypothesis that wages decentralized labor allocations. Suppose that this exercise was performed on two separate economies in which firms had identical production functions. In one economy workers are risk averse with preferences given by $U(c-kh)$ and firms are risk neutral. In the other economy, workers' preferences are given by $c-kh$ while firms are risk averse. As discussed earlier in this section, these two economies produce identical hours schedules (as a function of the state) but very different compensation patterns. Under the hypothesis that wages decentralized hours decisions, the econometrician would be led to rather different estimates of technology under these two economies.

From a theoretical perspective, it is useful to consider the extent to which contracting models differ from the Arrow–Debreu complete contingent markets paradigm. In some cases, one can think of labor contracts as one of (potentially) many agreements which together create complete markets. That is, the presence of labor contracts, per se, need not signal anything about the incompleteness of markets. This is the view taken in Wright [95]. For example, the fact that a risk neutral firm rather than a risk neutral insurance company provides insurance to its worker, may have no allocative consequences. Alternatively, if risks must be borne by risk averse firms rather than risk neutral insurance companies, (perhaps because of incentive problems), then the contracting model will differ from the complete markets setting.

It should also be noted that the contracts studied thus far have been unrestricted in that all terms of the agreement were freely contingent on all events. One common way to move away from the complete markets model is to consider (as we do in the next section) restrictions on information which limit the set of feasible contracts directly.

Before moving to that topic, it is useful to think about the relationship of the contract to the underlying labor market. In the contracting problem described earlier, we took as given the firms' workforce, N, and the level of expected utility, $\bar{U}$, available to workers outside the firm. The reason for this was our interest in the form of the labor contract rather than the ex ante allocation of workers. Presumably, $\bar{U}$ and N are determined in an ex ante market for workers. As $\bar{U}$ varies, this traces out ex ante labor supply and labor demand schedules for workers and firms respectively. The equilibrium $\bar{U}$ clears this ex ante market. Thus the initial matching of workers and firms could be achieved in an auction setting with the contract governing the behavior of the agents thereafter.[9] The discussion of Azariadis's [3] contracting model in the next section illustrates this approach to closing the model.

3. RESTRICTED CONTRACTS: MISSING CONTINGENCIES, ASYMMETRIC INFORMATION AND ENFORCEMENT PROBLEMS

The contracting models studied thus far have illustrated the rich possibilities for employment and wage compensation variations consistent with this approach. For economists interested in understanding divergent patterns of employment and compensation, these results are certainly of interest. However, since its inception, the contracting approach has sought to provide insight into a number of inefficiencies believed to characterize employment relations. From this perspective, the basic model exhibited above is not very enlightening.

To remedy this, we now turn to a consideration of contracting models which constrain the behavior of agents in a variety of ways

[9] If contracts were complete, then the single market meeting would be sufficient to reproduce the complete markets solution even though the contract is a bilateral agreement.

and can lead to such interesting phenomena as inefficient job separations and inefficiencies in hours of work and wage profiles. The first two inefficiencies are created by relaxing the assumptions made in the basic model about costless observation by both parties of the state of nature and the costless inclusion of contingencies in the contract. In these models, contingencies within the contract are absent altogether or are present at the cost of incentive compatibility. The third phenomena, wage profiles, is driven by problems with enforcing labor contracts. In an intertemporal setting, the enforcement problem generates wage profiles as part of an incentive package to retain workers. We also briefly consider enforcement problems created by asymmetric information between the contractants and the courts.

We begin this section with an exposition of the contracting model first explored in Azariadis [3]. This model highlights the implications of missing severance payments for the pattern of layoffs. We then focus on the implications of asymmetric information for contracting and discuss some of the distortions generated in optimal contracts. The final part of the section focuses on enforcement problems.

Layoffs with restrictions on severance pay

This section relies quite heavily on Azariadis [3] which was one of the first papers, along with Baily [8] and Gordon [38], to explain the implications of risk sharing for employment relations. The approach taken by Azariadis differs from the basic model in a number of critical ways. First, the model does not allow worksharing so that variations in total hours corresponds to variations in employment. The implications of this technological restriction were studied briefly in Section 2. Second, the model does not allow contracts to include severance payments from firms to workers in the event of layoffs. Unlike the technological restriction, this prohibition on severance payment is a constraint directly on the optimal contract. Below, we discuss the possible restrictions on information that could help justify this exclusion of severance payments.

Suppose, then, we consider the optimal contract between a risk-neutral firm and a group of N identical risk averse workers. We will treat N as endogenous in this exercise. Each worker is endowed with one indivisible unit of time which is either supplied to the firm or consumed directly by the worker. The utility of an employed worker is $U(w)$ where w is total compensation. An unemployed worker receives $U(k)$ where k can be thought of as the worker's value of time (in consumption units) and/or any severance payments (unemployment insurance) received from the *government.* We assume that $U(.)$ is strictly increasing and strictly concave. This preference structure is identical to the case of perfect substitutes explored earlier (with the additional restriction on worksharing).

The firm's profit in state s, $\pi(s)$, is given by

$$\pi(s) = sf(L(s)) - w(s)L(s) \tag{8}$$

where $L(s)$ is the number of employed workers. As before, we also use $\rho(s) \equiv L(s)/N$ as the probability an aribtrary worker is employed in state s. The production function, $f(\cdot)$, is strictly increasing and strictly concave.

Taking $\bar{U}$ as the market determined expected utility constraint on obtaining workers, the optimal contract, $\{w^*(s), \rho^*(s), N\}$

$$\text{maximizes } E_s\pi(s)$$

subject to

$$E_s\{\rho(s)U(w(s)) + (1-\rho(s))U(k)\} \geq \bar{U}, \tag{9}$$

$$1 \geq \rho(s) \quad \text{for all } s, \tag{10}$$

and

$$\rho(s) \geq 0 \quad \text{for all } s. \tag{11}$$

Denote, by $\gamma^*(\bar{U}, k)$, the solution to this optimization problem. Let λ denote the multiplier associated with (9) and let $\beta(s)$ be the multiplier associated with (10) in state s. We assume that $f'(L) \to \infty$ as $L \to 0$ so that (11) will never bind. The first-order conditions with respect to $w(s)$ and $\rho(s)$ correspond to (2)–(4) with the added restrictions that $w^u(s) = 0$ and $h(s) = 1$ for all s. They are:

$$U'(w(s)) = N/\lambda \quad \text{for all } s, \tag{12}$$

and

$$sf'(\rho(s)N) = w(s) - \frac{U(w(s)) - U(k)}{U'(w(s))} + \beta(s) \quad \text{for all } s. \tag{13}$$

The first expression corresponds to the conditions for efficient risk sharing (given the restrictions on the contract) in states of employment. From the assumed risk neutrality of the firm, (12) implies that the employment wage, $w(s)$, is state independent: i.e. $w(s) = \bar{w}$ for all s. Expression (13), given that $w(s) = \bar{w}$, determines the level of employment in state s. If $\beta(s) > 0$, then $\rho(s) = 1$ in state s. The employment probability, $\rho(s)$, is increasing in s and is strictly increasing over the range of s where $\rho(s) < 1$.[10]

As discussed above, the left-hand side of (13) is the firm's gain from hiring another worker while the right-hand side expresses the cost. The direct wage cost is given by $\bar{w}$. The second term is a risk premium for the employment risk generated by $U(\bar{w}) - U(k)$. Since $\bar{U} > U(k)$ is a property (discussed below) of the equilibrium in the ex ante labor market, we see that $U(\bar{w}) > U(k)$. The firm therefore benefits from employing another worker by reducing the employment risk. That is, if $\rho(s)$ is increased in some state, $\bar{w}$ can be reduced so that (9) is maintained with equality. Hence, in the optimal contract there emerges a tradeoff between the level of compensation ($\bar{w}$) and the amount of employment risk faced by workers, $\rho(s)$.

The first-order condition with respect to N is

$$E_s\rho(s)sf'(\rho(s)N) - E_s\rho(s)\bar{w} = 0. \tag{14}$$

This is interpreted as equating the expected marginal benefit and cost of adding another worker to the workforce.

A main contribution of Azariadis's paper was a characterization of the circumstances under which $\rho(s) < 1$ emerged in an optimal contract. To start, suppose we find the optimal full employment contract: i.e. set $\rho(s) = 1$ for all s. From (9) and (12), $w^f = U^{-1}(\bar{U})$ where w^f is the full employment wage paid to workers. In this contract, the workers are fully insured against shocks to the firm's technology: neither their compensation nor employment status depends on $\tilde{s}$. Yet, because of our restriction against severance pay, this complete insurance by the firm requires that $L(s) = N$ for all s. This is potentially costly to the firm since it is unable to reduce employment in adverse states of nature. So the full-employment contract may be dominated by one allowing layoffs. Whether or not layoffs arise in an optimal contract will ultimately depend on the

[10] When $\beta(s) = 0$, $sf'(\rho(s)N)$ is a constant so that $\rho'(s) > 0$. Let $\hat{s}$ be the smallest s for which $\beta(s) > 0$. Then $\beta(s) > 0$ for all $s > \hat{s}$ and hence $\rho(s) = 1$ for all $s \geq \hat{s}$.

size of the risk premium,

$$\frac{U(w)-U(k)}{U'(w)} \equiv \eta(w, k)$$

and the firm's desire to vary employment in low productivity states. Note that $\eta(w, k)$ is a decreasing function of k and an increasing function both of the worker's degree of absolute risk aversion and w.[11]

Given the monotonicity of $\rho(s)$, we can check to see if the full employment contract can be dominated by one allowing layoffs in the lowest state, $\underline{s}$. If it cannot be dominated, then the full employment contract is an optimal contract.

Borrowing a diagram from [6], Figure 1 shows the indifference curves between $\rho(\underline{s})$ and $\bar{w}$ for workers and firms. The slope of the worker's indifference curve is

$$-p(\underline{s})\frac{[U(\bar{w})-U(k)]}{E_s\rho(s)U'(\bar{w})} = \frac{-\eta(\bar{w}, k)}{E_s\rho(s)} \tag{15}$$

while the slope for the firm is

$$p(\underline{s})\frac{(\underline{s}f'(\underline{s}N)-\bar{w})}{E_s\rho(s)} \tag{16}$$

where $p(\underline{s})$ is the probability that $\tilde{s}=\underline{s}$. The preferred sets for the contractants, relative to the point $(1, w^f)$ are shaded in the figure. It is possible to Pareto dominate a full-employment contract if and only if the slope of the workers' indifference curve is less (in absolute value) than the firm's at the point $(1, w^f)$. That is, a necessary and sufficient condition for layoffs when $\underline{s}$ occurs is

$$\underline{s}f'(N)-w^f < -\frac{[U(w^f)-U(k)]}{U'(w^f)} = -\eta(w^f, k) \tag{17}$$

since $\rho(s)=1$ for all s if $\rho(\underline{s})=1$. This is the case displayed in Figure 1. That is, layoffs occur if the firm is willing to pay more to

[11] From a second-order approximation of $u(\cdot)$, we see that

$$\eta(\bar{w}, k) \approx \bar{w}-k+\frac{(\bar{w}-k)^2}{2}A(\bar{w})$$

where $A(\bar{w}) \equiv -u''(\bar{w})/u'(\bar{w})$ is the Arrow–Pratt measure of absolute risk aversion.

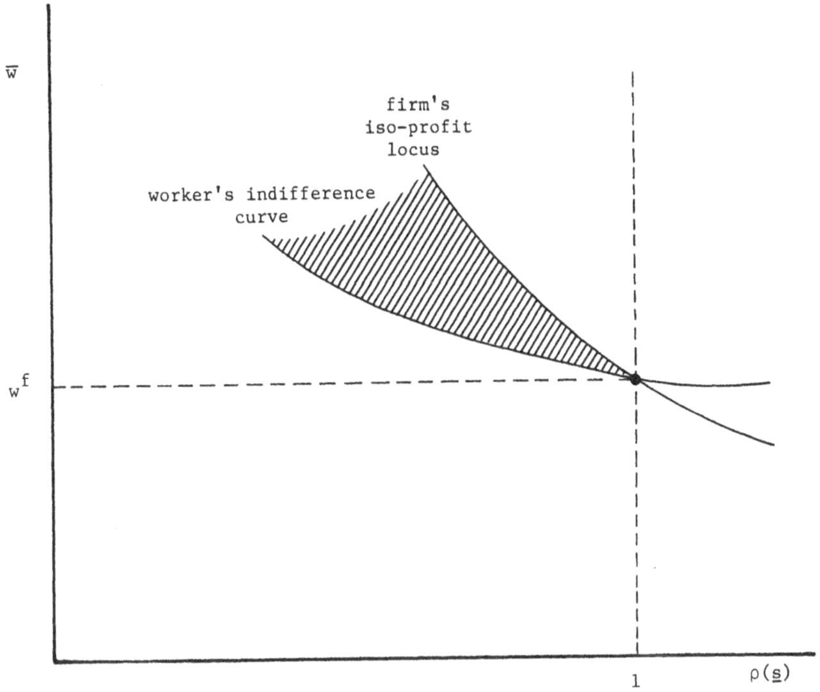

FIGURE 1 Optimal contract with layoffs.

the workers to reduce the level of employment, in the lowest state, than the workers require as compensation for the extra employment risk.

From (17) layoffs are more likely: the smaller is $\underline{s}$ and the smaller is the worker's risk premium. As k falls or the workers become more risk averse, the likelihood of layoffs falls since they require more compensation to absorb a little employment risk.

With $\rho(\underline{s})<1$, $\beta(s)=0$ for s close to $\underline{s}$ and (13) will characterize the level of employment in each of the unemployment states. In state $\bar{s}$, $\rho(\bar{s})=1$ so that all N members of the firm's workforce are employed. If $\rho(\bar{s})<1$, the firm could profitably increase $E\pi(s)$ without violating (9).

The effect of $U(k)$ on the optimal solution to this contracting problem provides for a number of interesting extensions of this model. First, if k reflects publicly provided unemployment insurance (UI), then it is clear that this government policy has an impact on the structure of the optimal contract.[12] Increases in UI reduce the costs of layoffs and therefore make them more likely.

Second, in a more complete model of the behavior of laid-off workers we might want to include the search decisions of these agents. We might also allow firms to hire additional workers ex post. As discussed in a recent paper by Hosios [59], this creates a situation in which the hiring and layoff policies of all firms are related, since these decisions influence the expected utility of a laid-off worker who is searching. This setting also allows macroeconomic variables—such as an unemployment rate—to affect the design of labor contracts through their effects on the expected payoff of unemployed workers.

An equilibrium for Azariadis's model is then obtained by finding the level of $\bar{U}$ such that the contractual labor market clears ex ante. Assuming there is free entry into the industry, at the market clearing level of expected utility the optimal contract will generate the same level of expected profits for the firm as they received in the spot market solution. Let U^s be the workers' expected utility from the spot market allocation in which they receive their marginal product in each state of nature. We assume that $\bar{s}$ is large enough that the spot market wage exceeds k in some state of nature so that $U^s > U(k)$. We also know that $\bar{U} \geq U^s$ as the spot market solution is a feasible contract. Hence $\bar{U} > U(k)$ and $\bar{w} > k$ as assumed in the analysis. Unemployed workers received lower utility than employed workers. If $U^s = U(k)$, then workers obtain smoothed consumption from the spot market allocation and contracts are not needed to shift risks.

In sum, Azariadis's model generates the possibility of layoffs in adverse states of nature. Due to the lack of severance pay, unemployed workers are worse-off than their identical counterparts at the firm. This asymmetry between the outcomes of identical agents could be overcome if worksharing were feasible. As Proposition 1 shows, these workers would accept variations in hours as a means of sharing this risk among themselves.

[12] See, for example Feldstein [29].

Azariadis's model has been criticized in a couple of ways. First, in the optimal contract, employment is higher than in the corresponding spot market solution. Suppose that, in some low state of nature $\hat{s}$, less than N workers would be hired by each firm in the spot market equilibrium. Then, the real wage would be driven down to k and employment per firm in a spot labor market (L^s) would satisfy

$$\hat{s}f'(L^s) = k. \tag{18}$$

In contrast, the employment level prescribed in an optimal contract (L^c) for state $\hat{s}$, is given by

$$\hat{s}f'(L^c) = \bar{w} - \frac{[U(\bar{w}) - U(k)]}{U'(\bar{w})}, \tag{19}$$

if $L^c < N$. Of course, if $L^c = N$, then we immediately see that employment is higher in the contract. Given that $U(\cdot)$ is strictly concave

$$\bar{w} - \frac{[U(\bar{w}) - U(k)]}{U'(\bar{w})} < k.$$

Hence $L^s < L^c$ is state $\hat{s}$. This result of "overemployment" is not surprising since the contractants substitute for the missing insurance contained in severance pay by stabilizing employment relative to the spot market allocation.

This result of contract employment in excess of spot market employment is often viewed as a weakness of this model. The argument, as I understand it, is that the model, while generating layoffs, cannot help us to understand an economy caught in an equilibrium with a low-level of employment and output. However, since the model itself is only one of a partial equilibrium, this criticism is not too troubling. It may be the case that once this contracting model is placed into a general equilibrium setting, employment and output could be depressed relative to the complete markets model.

A deeper criticism concerns the missing severance payments. The model focuses on the implications of a restriction in an optimal contract without providing an explanation for it. This is comparable to focusing on the implications of incomplete contingent market general equilibrium models without a good theory of missing markets. A more useful (but harder) approach, would be to derive the missing severance payments as a consequence of information problems. We will return to this issue at the end of the following section on contracting with imperfect information.

Employment distortions and information asymmetries

In considering the contracts studied thus far, one is struck by their informational requirements. As the problem has been formulated, the parties to a contract agree, ex ante, on the distribution of the shock to the firm's technology and then, ex post, costlessly observe the realized value of the shock. The reasonableness of these assumptions depends, ultimately, on the interpretation that is given to the random variable, $\tilde{s}$. If this shock, as an example, represents the amount of rainfall within a prescribed period, then both parties to the contract could observe the current state as well as the rainfall history. Alternatively, the worker may have little information about a firm's technological history so that our assumption that the ex ante distribution of $\tilde{s}$ is common knowledge may be too severe. Similarly, we could think of the firm's profit function as being a reduced form expression in which all of the other choice variables have been optimized out. In this case the random variable $\tilde{s}$ represents the myriad of random events in other aspects of the firm's operations influencing its profit function defined solely over labor. It then seems quite reasonable that the firm is better informed about realizations of s than are workers.

Starting with this view, the papers by Calvo–Phelps [18] and Hall–Lilien [48] began to explore the implications of imperfect information on the design of labor contracts. These early efforts stimulated further research by Azariadis [7], Chari [20], Cooper [21], Green–Kahn [42], Grossman–Hart [44, 45] and many others. The activity in this area, as we will see below, was driven by the prior understanding that apparent ex post inefficiencies (such as inefficient employment decisions) could be part of an optimal, ex ante, arrangement in the presence of informational asymmetries.

To explore these issues, we start with a variant of the basic model. Suppose there is a single firm with profits in state s described by

$$\pi(s) = sf(h) - w.$$

The firm's preferences over $\pi(s)$ are represented by a Von-Neumann Morgenstern utility functions, $V(\pi(s))$, where $V(\cdot)$ is strictly increasing and concave. The variable h is hours worked and w is total compensation.

Further, suppose there is a single worker with preferences represented by $U(w, h; \tilde{\theta})$. Here $\tilde{\theta}$ represents a shock to the worker's preferences over consumption and labor time. Assume $\tilde{\theta} \in [\underline{\theta}, \bar{\theta}]$. We discuss some interpretations of $\tilde{\theta}$ below.

If hours worked vary continuously in $[0, 1]$ and ex post realizations of (s, θ) are observable to *both* parties, then the optimal contract, $\delta^* = \{w^*(s, \theta), h^*(s, \theta)\}$, maximizes

$$E_{s,\theta} V(\pi(s, \theta))$$
$$\text{subject to } E_{s,\theta} U(w, h; \theta) \geq \bar{U},$$

where $E_{s,\theta}$ is the expectation over both $\tilde{s}$ and $\tilde{\theta}$. Note that the firm's profits depend on realizations of both s *and* θ to the extent that either compensation or hours worked depends on these random variables.

The optimal contract satisfies

$$\lambda U_w(w, h, \theta) = V'(sf(h) - w), \tag{20}$$

and

$$\lambda U_h(w, h, \theta) = V'(sf(h) - w)sf'(h) \quad \text{for all } (s, \theta), \tag{21}$$

where λ is a Lagrange multiplier. These are the first-order conditions assuming we have an interior solution for all (s, θ). Equations (20) and (21) again express the conditions for optimal risk sharing and productive efficiency.

Using this contract as a starting point, we can begin to explore the implications of imperfect information about realizations of $\tilde{s}$ and/or $\tilde{\theta}$. We start with the problem of a firm which is better informed about realizations of $\tilde{s}$ than are workers. We then consider alternative specifications of the information structure.

(*i*) *Firms have superior information.* Suppose that realizations of the random variable $\tilde{s}$ are observable to the firm but not to its workers. This is an extreme case of the situation in which the firm is better informed. At this stage we can either assume that realizations of $\tilde{\theta}$ are publicly observable or assume that $\tilde{\theta}$ is degenerate. To save on notation, we assume that the latter holds and represent workers' preferences by $U(w, h)$ with the properties asserted earlier.

At the time of contract negotiation, the workers know that, ex post, the firm will have superior information about $\tilde{s}$. How, then, are contracts implemented ex post and how does the firm's superior information influence the contract which is chosen ex ante?

The approach to addressing these questions was developed in the literature on the design of incentive compatible mechanisms. With regards to ex post implementation, we can simply think of the firm being asked to announce a feasible state of nature (i.e. an s within $[\underline{s}, \bar{s}]$). Given an arbitrary contract $(w(s), h(s))$, the announced state is used to determine compensation and hours. This form of implementation is known as a *direct revelation mechanism.*

Consider an arbitrary contract, $\delta(s)$. Workers know, ex post, that the firm will announce a state which maximizes its profits, given $\delta(s)$. Hence, in terms of the *realized* levels of compensation and employment, $\delta(s)$ is equivalent to another contract, call it $\hat{\delta}(s)$, with the property that the firm will announce the true state when faced with $\hat{\delta}(s)$.[13] Therefore there is no loss in generality, given the rationality of workers, in confining attention to contracts under which firms have no incentive to misreport the true state of nature: i.e. to *incentive compatible contracts.* This is the crux of the revelation principle developed by Myerson [75] and Harris–Townsend [51].

To formally restrict the set of feasible contracts to those which are incentive compatible, we need to add conditions for truthtelling to our optimization problem. Let $\pi(s/\hat{s})$ represent the firm's profits if it announces that the realized value of $\tilde{s}$ is s when the true value is $\hat{s}$. That is

$$\pi(s/\hat{s}) = \hat{s}f(h(s)) - w(s),$$

where $(w(s), h(s))$ correspond to the levels of compensation and employment for state s in some arbitrary contract. Hence truthtelling by firms requires that, for all realized values of $\hat{s} \in [\underline{s}, \bar{s}]$,

$$\pi(\hat{s}/\hat{s}) \geq \pi(s/\hat{s}) \quad \text{for all } s \in [\underline{s}, \bar{s}]. \tag{22}$$

[13] $\hat{\delta}(s)$ is constructed from $\delta(s)$ by looking at the firm's announced state, under $\delta(s)$, if state s occurs. Call this announcement function, $m(s)$. So if $\delta(s) \equiv \{w(s), h(s)\}$, then $\hat{\delta}(s) \equiv \{w(m(s)), h(m(s))\}$.

So, in an incentive compatible contract, the firm must be willing to tell the truth in *all possible states* rather than to lie and announce *any other feasible state*. Any contract satisfying these incentive compatibility conditions is termed *implementable*.

Adding (22) restricts the set of feasible contracts. Hence, it is unlikely (though possible) that the optimal contract δ^* will satisfy (22). To investigate this issue and to see how the addition of (22) influences employment and compensation patterns, we consider some special cases.

Suppose, to start, that the firm is risk neutral, so that $V''(\cdot) \equiv 0$. With δ^* described by (20) and (21), (when $\tilde{\theta}$ is degenerate), we ask whether or not it satisfies (22): i.e., is δ^* implementable? Since $\tilde{s}$ is a continuous random variable, δ^* is implementable if

$$sf'(h^*(s))\frac{dh^*(s)}{ds} = \frac{dw^*(s)}{ds}. \tag{23}$$

When (23) holds, the firm has no incentive to misrepresent the state of nature. We can derive $dh^*(s)/ds$ and $dw^*(s)/ds$ from (20) and (21). Expressions (23) then becomes

$$(U_h/U_w)U_{ww} - U_{wh} = 0 \tag{24}$$

where these derivatives of the worker's utility function are evaluated at $(w^*(s), h^*(s))$ for $s \in [\underline{s}, \bar{s}]$. If (24) holds then δ^* is implementable. If (24) fails in *any* state, then δ^* is not incentive compatible.

Condition (24) is equivalent to the condition that the demand for leisure is independent of income.[14] One representation of preferences satisfying this condition was explored in Section 2. When leisure and consumption are perfect substitutes (i.e. $U(w, h) = U(w - kh)$), then (24) holds and δ^* is implementable. If the left

---

[14] That is, suppose a worker solves a labor supply problem, maximize$_h$ $U(wh + y, h)$ where w is a *wage rate* and y is outside income. If $h^*(w, y)$ is the solution, then

$$\frac{\partial h^*}{\partial y}(w, y) = \frac{-U_{cc}\dfrac{U_h}{U_c} + U_{ch}}{-[w^2U_{cc} + 2wU_{ch} + U_{hh}]}.$$

Here the subscript c refers to derivatives with respect to the first argument of $U(\cdot)$. With $U(\cdot)$ quasi-concave, the sign of $\partial h/\partial y$ is determined by the numerator. Leisure demand is independent of income when the numerator equals zero as in (24). Leisure is a normal (inferior) good when the numerator is negative (positve).

side of (24) is positive (negative), then leisure is a normal (inferior) good. In either case, δ^* is not implementable.

What is it about preferences satisfying (24) that ensures the implementability of δ^*? From (23), we know that compensation must increase with the state at a rate which is sufficient to offset the firm's desire (from Proposition 2) to increase employment (and hence profits) by announcing a high state of nature. When leisure and consumption are perfect substitutes, so that (24) is met, the workers' level of utility is state independent (from (20)) *and* the contractants' marginal rates of substitution are equalized in each state. (See Figure 2.) Hence the contract δ^* is simply implement-

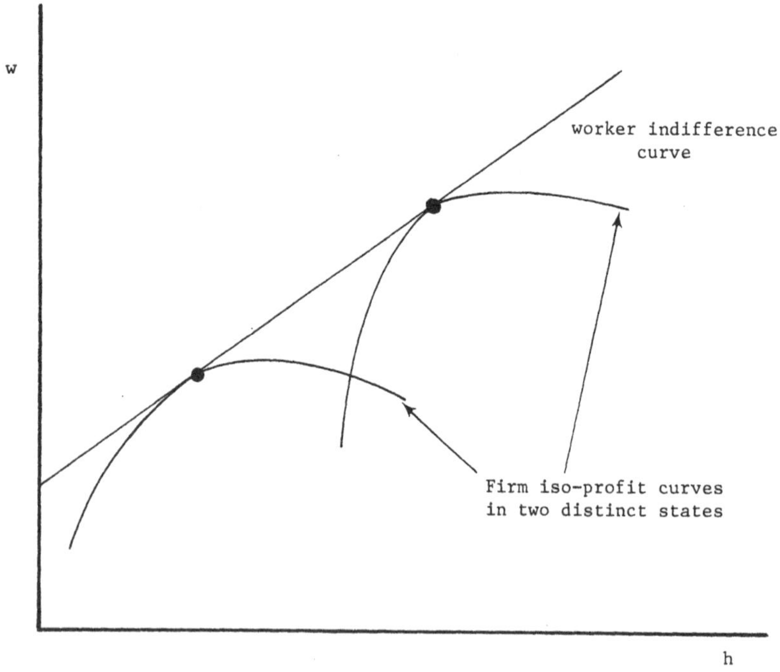

FIGURE 2 Consumption and hours are perfect substitutes.

able by allowing the firm to choose (w, h) along the worker's $\bar{U}$ indifference curve.

The case of perfect substitutes is thus very special. In general (24) will not be met and δ^* will not be implementable. Given that, we return to our optimization problem to characterize the optimal contract in an environment of asymmetric information.

To determine the optimal contract, we consider the problem of

$$\text{maximize } E_s \pi(s) \tag{25}$$

subject to

$$E_s U(w(s), h(s)) \geq \bar{U}$$

and (22).

The key issue in solving this problem is to determine which of the incentive compatibility conditions in (22) are binding. There is also the related issue of expressing (22) in a tractable fashion. If $\tilde{s}$ is discrete and takes on N values, then (22) is a set of $N(N-1)$ inequalities which may be difficult to handle. If $\tilde{s}$ is continuous, then (22) can be replaced by the necessary and sufficient conditions for an optimum (as discussed in Appendix B). The latter case was treated in [42] and [21].

PROPOSITION 3 *In the solution to* (25), *if leisure is a normal good in workers' preferences then*

$$sf'(h(s)) < \frac{-U_h(w(s), h(s))}{U_w(w(s), h(s))} \quad \textit{for} \quad s \in (\underline{s}, \bar{s}). \tag{26}$$

If leisure is an inferior good, then

$$sf'(h(s)) > \frac{-U_h(w(s), h(s))}{U_w(w(s), h(s))} \quad \textit{for} \quad s \in (\underline{s}, \bar{s}). \tag{27}$$

Proof See Appendix B.

This proposition provides a connection between properties of workers' preferences and the form of employment distortions that may arise in the solution to (25). When leisure is either a normal or an inferior good, the firm has an incentive to misrepresent the true state when faced with δ^*. To prevent this misrepresentation, the terms of the contract adjust to induce truthtelling. The costs of creating these incentives take two forms: first, risk-sharing is a sub-optimal (relative to δ^*) and second, marginal rates of substitution are not equalized, *ex post.* From Proposition 3, if leisure is normal then the distortion appears as overemployment (from (26)) while the opposite case of underemployment occurs when leisure is inferior (27).

Figure 3 displays these two cases. We term (26) an overemployment condition since, ex post, the contractants would be better off if

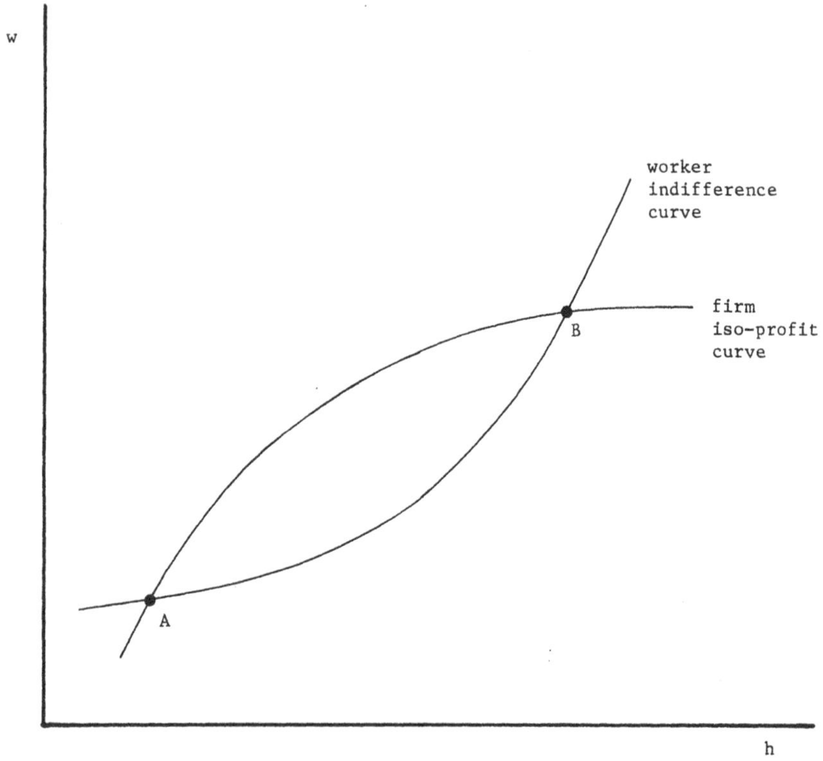

FIGURE 3 Employment distortions.

they reduced both compensation and hours. Equation (27) is similarly an underemployment condition since the parties can both enjoy gains from increasing both (w, h) ex post. In the figure, point A is one of underemployment while B is one of overemployment.

These ex post gains are, of course, recognized at the time of contracting. However, they are *not* realized in an optimal contract. The incentive compatibility conditions create an externality across the compensation and hours paid in each state. So adjusting (w, h) in a state of underemployment would have bad incentive effects in other states. The optimal contract balances ex post gains against these incentive effects *across* states.

The conditions for underemployment (i.e., the inferiority of leisure) seem a bit severe. To the extent that this theory was developed to help in explaining underemployment, Proposition 3 is disappointing. Underemployment is not a robust result when the firm is assumed to be risk neutral.

As mentioned earlier, there is also a theory of employment distortions when firms are risk averse developed in [7] and [44, 45]. To highlight the contribution of firm risk aversion to the underemployment result, we suppose that workers' preferences satisfy (24) so that consumption and leisure are perfect substitutes. Furthermore, we examine a model where worksharing is *not* feasible so that adjustments in employment take place by separations between the firm and the single worker. In this model, we also allow severance pay. Hence the model closely follows Grossman and Hart [44, 45].

Firm's preferences over profits are represented by $V(\pi(s))$ with $V' > 0$ and $V'' < 0$. If the worker is employed, profits are given by

$$\pi(s) = \tilde{s} - w^e(s),$$

where $\tilde{s}$ takes values between $\underline{s}$ and $\bar{s}$. If the worker is unemployed

$$\pi(s) = -w^u(s).$$

So $w^e(s)$ is a state-dependent level of compensation to the employed worker while $w^u(s)$ is the (potentially) state-dependent level of severance pay.

Workers' preferences, if employed, are represented by $w^e - k$ where $k \in (\underline{s}, \bar{s})$ is a (non-random) measure of the disutility of working. If the worker is not employed, then he/she receives w^u from the firm.

If $\tilde{s}$ was observable to both parties, the optimal contract would stipulate employment iff $s \geq k$. The risk neutral workers would completely insure the firm so that $s - w^e(s) = \bar{\pi} = -w^u(s)$. Hence $w^e(s)$ decreases with s while $w^u(s)$ is independent of s.

This contract is not incentive compatible if $\tilde{s}$ is not publicly observed. The firm can profit by understating the true value of $\tilde{s}$ to reduce $w^e(s)$. Hence, incentive compatibility requires that $w^e(s)$ and $w^u(s)$ both be state independent. This highlights an important aspect of incentive compatible contracts: they can be characterized by employment contingent compensation schedules where the firm has the right to determine the employment level, ex post. (This is, in fact, an equivalent way of representing the ex post implementation game.)[15]

In this model, the contract stipulates two numbers, w^e and w^u and an employment rule. Since the firm alone observes $\tilde{s}$, employment occurs when the firm gains from employing the worker, i.e., when

$$\tilde{s} \geq w^e - w^u.$$

Hence, one can characterize the contract as the selection of w^u and $\Delta^* \equiv w^e - w^u$ with employment occuring iff $s \geq \Delta^*$. If $\Delta^* > k$, then there are states with $\Delta^* > s > k$ in which not employment occurs. This is an underemployment inefficiency relative to the full information contract. Letting $F(s)$ be the distribution function of $\tilde{s}$, the optimal contract (w^{*u}, Δ^*) maximizes

$$\int_{\underline{s}}^{\Delta} V(-w^u)\, dF(s) + \int_{\Delta}^{\bar{s}} V(s - w^e)\, dF(s)$$

subject to

$$\int_{\underline{s}}^{\Delta} w^u + \int_{\Delta}^{\bar{s}} (w^e - k)\, dF(s) \geq \bar{U}.$$

[15] That is, one can convert from implementation through a direct revelation mechanism to a more intuitively appealing scheme under which the firm chooses employment along a schedule which relates compensation to employment levels. This is similar to non-linear pricing schemes and other schemes used in models of sorting.

Using this set-up Grossman–Hart [44] show:

PROPOSITION 4 *In the solution to this problem,*

$$\Delta^* > k.$$

Proof See [44].

Hence, if the firm is risk averse, unemployment—in that there are realizations of $s \in (k, \Delta^*)$ where employment does *not* occur—arises in the optimal contract. Intuitively, incentive compatibility requires that $w^e(s)$ be state-independent. As a consequence, employment states are risky for the firm while unemployment states are riskless. So, to substitute for the missing insurance opportunities, the parties agree to increase the number of *riskless* unemployment states. By raising Δ^* above k, insurance is improved while, for Δ^* sufficiently close to k, efficiency losses due to underemployment are relatively small.

It is, of course, possible to build on Propositions 3 and 4 to consider various combinations of degrees of firm risk aversion and workers' preferences to complete the characterization of employment distortions. It appears though that this theory is currently unable to deliver the prediction of unemployment as a robust result.[16] That is, one can always find reasonable combinations of worker and firm preferences to generate any desired pattern of distortions. Whether or not the restrictions on preferences necessary for unemployment are empirically relevant remains an open issue. We now turn to a consideration of alternative incentive problems affecting labor contracts.

(*ii*) *Workers have superior information.* The analysis, thus far, has focused on the contractural implications of firms being better informed than workers about realizations of $\tilde{s}$. Returning to the more general setting with random disturbances of $\tilde{s}$ to firms' technology and $\tilde{\theta}$ to workers' tastes, we can consider the implications of workers being better informed about realizations of $\tilde{\theta}$. For this exercise, we assume that $\tilde{s}$ is a degenerate random variable.

There are a number of cases where this approach, depending on the interpretation given to $\tilde{\theta}$, is interesting. First, we can view

[16] See Stiglitz [90] for elaboration.

realizations of $\tilde{\theta}$ as influencing a single worker's marginal rate of substitution between consumption and labor. In this case, the labor contract may play an insurance role in terms of sharing the risks of alternative values of $\tilde{\theta}$. Or, the firm could be viewed as contracting with a worker whose value of $\tilde{\theta}$ has been determined but is not observed by the firm. The optimal contract is then a mechanism for extracting surplus from workers with unobservable tastes.

Second, we could also view $\tilde{\theta}$ as an indicator of workers' alternatives outside of the firm. This interpretation is more appropriate when layoffs are present and workers obtain job offers from other firms. The private information assumption seems reasonable in that a firm is unlikely to be informed about the alternatives of its unemployed workers. Realizations of $\tilde{\theta}$ are important to the contractants to the extent that optimal severance payments could be dependent upon it.[17]

To address the first of these interpretations, we simply add the appropriate incentive compatibility conditions to ensure that the worker truthfully reveals $\tilde{\theta}$. An arbitrary contract $\{w(\theta), h(\theta)\}$ is incentive compatible iff, for all $\hat{\theta} \in [\underline{\theta}, \bar{\theta}]$,

$$U(w(\hat{\theta}), h(\hat{\theta}); \hat{\theta}) \geq U(w(\theta), h(\theta); \theta) \quad \text{for all } \theta \in [\underline{\theta}, \bar{\theta}]. \tag{28}$$

This condition is the analogue of (22) for the case when workers are the better informed agents.

The optimal contract, when workers observe $\tilde{\theta}$ and firms do not, is determined by maximizing

$$E_\theta \pi(\theta) \tag{29}$$

subject to

$$E_\theta U(w(\theta), h(\theta); \theta) \geq \bar{U}$$

and (28).

In the objective function, $\pi(\cdot)$ depends on θ through its influence on the levels of w and h. The expected utility constraint is appropriate if we view $\tilde{\theta}$ as a random variable influencing a single worker's preferences when the contract is struck ex ante. (The sorting interpretation requires a slight variation of this problem.)

Moore [72] and Cooper [22] consider the solution to (29) under certain restrictions on workers' preferences. As is now well-known, in dealing with incentive constraints such as (28), it is useful that

[17] See Geanakoplos–Ito [35] for a model along these lines.

workers' marginal rate of substitution between (w, h) be a monotone function of θ. This restriction is often termed the *single-crossing property* since indifference curves (for different values of θ) cross only once. Assuming that the single-crossing property holds, allows us to simplify the incentive constraints for this problem.

PROPOSITION 5 *If workers' preferences satisfy the single-crossing property, $U_{w\theta}(\cdot) \geq 0$ and leisure is a normal good, then the solution to* (29) *displays underemployment for $\theta \in (\underline{\theta}, \bar{\theta})$.*

Proof See [22].

This result is closely tied to that obtained in standard self-selection models except that here we are sorting across the various possible types of a single-worker. As in those models, the requirement of incentive compatibility creates distortions is quantities which, in the contracting model, take the form of reduced hours.

Moore [72] and Cooper [22] also discuss the case in which leisure demand is independent of income (so that Proposition 5 does not apply). As discussed by these authors, and Hart [53] as well, the type of employment distortion depends critically on whether it is the value of leisure or the disutility of work which is random.

To understand this, consider two possible specifications of a worker's utility function:

$$U(w, h, \theta) = \hat{U}(w - \theta h) \tag{30}$$

$$U(w, h, \theta) = \hat{U}(w + \theta(1 - h)). \tag{31}$$

Suppose that workers are endowed with a unit of time and that worksharing is not feasible, so that $h \in \{0, 1\}$. In (30), the workers' disutility from working is random while, in (31), it is the value of leisure time which is random. Moore [72] interprets (30) as the case in which layoffs are temporary so that θ reflects the disutility of work while (31) pertains to permanent layoffs where θ represents an alternative wage.

If realizations of $\tilde{\theta}$ were observable to both the firm and its worker, then the optimal contract (for either specification of preferences) would guarantee the worker a constant level of utility for all θ. For preferences described by (30), the wage paid to the employed worker would vary with θ while, for (31), severance pay would depend on θ.

In the presence of asymmetric information, the contract can only stipulate two wage levels: w^e if $h=1$ and w^u if $h=0$. The employment distortions created by the informational asymmetry are then easy to see. When the disutility of work is random (as in (30)), the restriction that w^e be independent of θ implies that states of employment are risky for the worker. Hence the optimal contract creates less employment (relative to the full information contract) to provide insurance to workers. If preferences are described by (31) then unemployment states are risky since w^u is state independent so that overemployment results. The intuition here is quite similar to that for the results by Grossman–Hart [44, 45]. Formal statements of results along these lines can be found in [72] or [22].

Considering preference structures—such as (31)—in which workers' utility, if unemployed, is influenced by random events *outside* of the firm is an example of the second type of problem in which workers have superior information. This approach is useful for understanding restrictions on severance payments. The main critique of Azariadis's [3] model with layoffs was its, apparently ad hoc, restriction on severance payments. Empirically, it seems to be the case that severance payments are generally not sufficient to fully compensate workers for their periods of unemployment. It is therefore useful to investigate further the structure of severance payments to unemployed workers in the presence of private information.

To do so, we require a model in which layoffs occur: so that Proposition 1 does not hold. Hence, we again assume that work-sharing is not feasible. Then, from (2)–(4), we could determine the optimal structure of wages, severance payment and employment levels. For the model of Azariadis [3] explored above, the contractants would set severance pay so that workers were perfectly insured across employment states. As a consequence, layoffs would have no effect on levels of utility and employment levels would coincide with the spot market allocation. Yet, for the most part, it seems that layoffs are undesirable. How, then, can we amend the model to generate welfare losses from layoffs?

To accomplish this, we need to consider, in a bit more detail, the behavior of those who are laid-off. For the most part, one can distinguish between temporary and permanent layoffs. For the former, a worker is told that the job will be available again after a period of time while, for the latter, the job is simply gone.

Presumably, whether or not a layoff is temporary depends on the reason for the dismissal in the first place. Thus far, contracting models have concentrated more on permanent layoffs and we will as well.

A permanently laid-off worker has a number of options available. The worker must decide whether to search or not and, in the event that offers arrive, whether or not to accept them. From the perspective of the firm trying (as part of an ex ante contract) to provide layoff insurance through a scheme of severance payments, these decisions by the worker are observable only at a cost. Assuming that these costs are relatively large, the firm takes into account the effect its severance pay policy will have on subsequent worker search behavior. In this sense, we need to consider the moral hazard problems associated with search behavior in the design of the optimal contract. Furthermore, there are additional incentive problems associated with requesting that workers inform the firm of the wages they receive once a new job is taken. Hence, the design of an optimal severance pay package is encumbered by the numerous incentive problems associated with the behavior of laid-off workers.

Kahn [62] provides an analysis of optimal severance pay when the firm is unable to observe the outside opportunities of workers. The model used is close to that used by Azariadis [3], with the added assumption that the compensation received by unemployed workers (k) is a random variable. Realizations of $\tilde{k}$ are not observable to the firm and it is impossible for the firm to construct a mechanism to have the worker reveal this random variable.[18] The contract specifies employment wages and unemployment compensation as functions of the observable shock to the firm's technology but independent of $\tilde{k}$. The worker, to preserve incentive compatibility, chooses whether or not to work for a firm. The approach is also close to that of [22] and [72] with the added feature that firm's experience productivity shocks.

Kahn finds that the contract stipulates that the difference between compensation to employed workers and the level of severance pay will increase with the firm's technology shock. When workers are very productive at the firm, the increased spread between income

[18] No sorting can occur as the firm has no leverage to extract this information.

and severance pay provides the desired incentive for the worker to remain with a firm. Hence, one cost of having workers better informed about their outside opportunities is that full insurance is not optimal. As one might expect from our earlier discussion, whether or not unemployment arises again depends on the form of workers' preferences.

(*iii*) *Other incentive problems and a summary.* Besides the incentive problems mentioned here, there are others worth noting. First, it is possible to combine these two cases to discuss the situation of bilateral asymmetric information: see Hall–Lazear [49], Cooper [22] and Moore [72] for some attempts in this direction. When both parties have private information, the incentive compatibility conditions express the requirement that truthtelling by both parties be an equilibrium in the ex post implementation game. To make this precise, one must specify an equilibrium concept and take into account the correlation between the variables privately observed by the parties.

From the work by Riordan [81] on implementing contracts with bilateral asymmetric information, we know that if both parties to the contract are risk neutral, it is possible to devise a contract which is incentive compatible and allocates labor efficiently. These results are closely related to those on determining the level of public goods and the tax structure to finance them. Riordan's results use a sequential equilibrium concept where one party (say the workers) chooses the compensation rule (expressing wages for each level of employment) and the firm then chooses the employment level.

When the contractants are not risk neutral or this sequential mechanism is not feasible, then the efficient allocation of labor is generally not obtainable. A full characterization of the conditions for inefficient separations has not yet been derived.

This problem of bilateral asymmetric information is closely related to the problem of bargaining under asymmetric information. The conditions for truthtelling are the same. The critical difference, of course, is in the timing of the receipt of the information relative to the time the contract is negotiated. In the contracting approach, the terms of the arrangement are determined ex ante.

Another important incentive problem arises with regards to the work effort put forth by employed workers. This problem of moral hazard has been dealt with extensively in the literature on managerial incentives (e.g. Harris–Raviv [51], Holmstrom [56]). It has more recently been used by Shapiro–Stiglitz [88], Foster–Wu [34] and others to provide insight on the structuring of compensation packages and lay-off patterns to provide incentives for workers to supply effort. This approach generates the prediction of low levels of severance payments and unemployment equilibrium as a means of punishing workers who shirk. Yellen [96] provides a useful summary of this problem and other aspects of the emerging "efficiency-wage" theories.

Before concluding this section on imperfect information, it is worthwhile to summarize the salient points. The inclusion of incentive compatibility conditions in the design of labor contracts helps us to understand the existence of (apparent) inefficiencies in employment relations. These incentive requirements (i.e. (22) and (28)) also imply that compensation and employment levels will be positively correlated. This monotonicity property is a common feature of models with incentive compatibility requirements.

This approach to contracting has been criticized for the lack of robust results. In particular, the conditions for underemployment seem a bit strong. Despite this criticism (or in response to it), work continues on understanding the effects of imperfect information on contracts. Perhaps this reflects a common view that informational imperfections are a root cause of inefficiencies in contracts.

Enforcement problems

Returning to our general theme, the purpose of this section of the monograph is to explore possible restrictions on the contracts characterized in Section 2. Thus far, we have considered contracts, following [3], with restrictions on worksharing and severance pay. We also analyzed the implications of informational asymmetries on contract design. The final type of restriction we consider concerns the enforcement of contracts.

In the basic contracting problem, workers and firms were matched ex ante. Firms designed a contract to maximize their expected utility taking as given the constraint that workers receive a minimum level of utility, $\bar{U}$. After this initial matching, the workers(s)–firm pair separates only to the extent that layoffs were part of the optimal contract. While ex post incentives may have existed for either of the contractants to abrogate the contract, we assumed that the contract was binding.

It is useful though to consider the enforceability of these contracts a bit more closely. So far, we have treated these contracts as if they were explicitly written agreements enforceable by a court of law. This view is, in fact, contrary to that taken in the early contracting models where the agreements were viewed as implicit in nature. If contracts are implicit, why do parties abide by their terms?

Reputation effects are one possible mechanism for enforcement. A firm which reneged on a contract with its workforce would be "punished" by having to pay higher wages to attract workers in the future. Workers would also gain reputations as "quitters" and hence find employment more difficult to obtain. In the absence of strong reputation effects, intertemporal incentives can also be established to ensure that the contractants abide by the terms of their implicit arrangement.

To understand this set of issues, we first need to understand the relationship between the contracting parties and the enforcing agent (the court). What, if anything, can the court observe about the contracting parties? What powers do the courts have? Once we model this enforcement relationship, we can then turn attention to the design of an optimal contract. At this stage, the contracting literature has yet to systematically address all of these issues. Nonetheless, there are some enlightening papers which provide some helpful insights.

To begin, consider amending the basic contracting model to reflect the (exogenous) legal restriction against involuntary servitude. That is, a worker cannot be bound by a contract to work for a firm if the worker wishes to abrograte the contract (i.e. quit).

This, of course, presents a big problem for the design of insurance schemes within the confines of a labor contract. In some states of nature, a worker receives a wage which exceeds his/her marginal product. This is a type of insurance indemnity in the optimal labor contract. In other states, a worker receives a wage below marginal product: this is the insurance premium. (So, for example, in [3], we found that the full employment wage satisfied $w^f = Es$.)

Suppose that the worker was not bound by the employment contract. Further assume that other firms experience the same shocks to their technology and that there is a well-functioning spot market for labor operating ex post. So, a worker receiving a wage below his/her marginal product outside of the firm could simply walk away from the labor contract instead of paying an insurance premium. As a consequence, the insurance aspect of the labor contract becomes infeasible since the worker cannot be forced to pay the premium.

Recent work by Holmstrom [58] and Ioannides–Pissarides [60] provides an answer to this problem through multiperiod contracting. Suppose, as an example, that the worker and firm can contract for two periods. The worker's productivity at the firm is random in the second period but not in the first. The compensation package negotiated within the optimal contract provides insurance to the worker against fluctuations in his/her second period marginal product. If the worker is not bound to remain with the firm in the second period, is there still a way for the firm to collect a premium for the implicit insurance embodied in the second period wage?

The answer given by Holmstrom and Ioannides–Pissarides is yes. The firm can collect the premium in the first period by paying the worker less than marginal product. This process, often called bonding, can generate a wage profile which is steeper than workers' productivity. This argument also predicts the use of senority layoff rules. Hence, the modification of the contracting model, made explicit below, brings us closer to some stylized facts of the labor market.

Consider a simple model which incorporates the key features of these papers. Let workers and firms co-exist for two periods. The first period of attachment is a training period and the worker's productivity equals unity with probability one. In the second period, the worker's productivity, if he/she remains with the initial firm, equals $\tilde{s} + \varepsilon$. Here $\tilde{s}$ is a random variable with $E\tilde{s} = 1$ and $\tilde{s} \in [\underline{s}, \bar{s}]$. The term ε is positive and measures *firm specific* training. If a worker leaves the firm in the second period, the worker receives $\tilde{s}$ (his/her marginal product *outside* of the firm) on the spot market. Hence, ε is lost to the worker-firm pair if the worker separates from the firm after the training period.

If contracts are fully enforceable on both parties, the optimal arrangement would stipulate that no ex post separations occur. The level of compensation paid to the workers is determined by

$$\underset{w_1, w_2(s)}{\text{Maximize}}\ U(w_1) + \frac{E_s U(w_2(s))}{1+\delta} \tag{32}$$

$$\text{subject to } (1 - w_1) + \frac{E_s(s + \varepsilon - w_2(s))}{1+r} = 0. \tag{33}$$

In the objective function, we have workers' expected utility over this two-period lifetime. Consistent with our discussion earlier that workers have restricted use of capital markets, (32) stipulates that compensation and consumption are the same. Workers discount future utility by $1/(1+\delta)$. Equation (33) is the expected discounted profits constraint for the firm where r is the market rate of interest. Ex ante competition for workers will ensure that (33) is met. The optimal compensation in period 2 is state-independent and satisfies

$$U'(w_1) = \frac{1+r}{1+\delta} U'(w_2). \tag{34}$$

So optimal insurance dictates that $w_2(s)$ be a constant while the relationship between r and δ determines the intertemporal pattern of compensation and hence consumption. With workers unable to either obtain insurance or operate in the capital market, the firm acts as an insurance broker, a banker and an employer.[19]

Suppose, now, that workers cannot be bound to a contract. That is, if their second-period productivity outside of the firm ($\bar{s}$) exceeds their wage, they can (and will) quit. To model this additional constraint, we add the requirement that

$$w_2(s) \geq s \quad \text{for all } s \tag{35}$$

to the original programming problem.

The combinations of (w_1, w_2) satisfying (33) and (34) will generally violate (35). If, as an example, $\delta = r$, (33) and (34) imply that

[19] See Hall [47] for a further discussion of this interpretation.

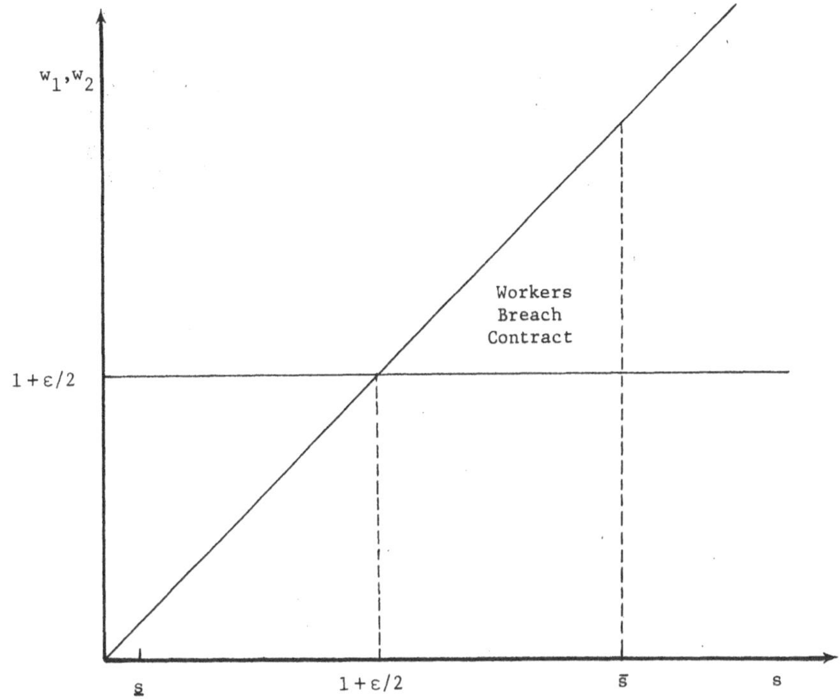

FIGURE 4 Workers breach of contract.

$w_1 = w_2 = 1 + \varepsilon/2 \equiv \bar{w}$. Hence, if $\bar{s} > 1 + \varepsilon/2$, then (35) will be violated. Of course, the gains to firm specific training could be so large, relative to the upper support of $\tilde{s}$, that the enforcement problem doesn't arise (i.e. $\bar{s} \leq 1 + \varepsilon/2$). Figure 4 illustrates a case in which $1 + \varepsilon/2 < \bar{s}$ so that the worker would breach the contract for $\tilde{s} \in (1 + \varepsilon/2, \bar{s}]$.

To understand the implications of adding (35) to the contract design problem, assume that $\delta = r$ and that $\bar{s} > 1 + \varepsilon/2$. With $\varepsilon > 0$, the worker and firm will always contract to ensure that no separations occur. As we will see, in high productivity states, the worker will receive compensation of $\tilde{s}$. Workers will be insured against low $\tilde{s}$ and pay an insurance premium through a reduced level of w_1.

Once we add (35) to the contracting problem, we need to determine the states for which this constraint is binding. It is not difficult to demonstrate that in the optimal contract there will be a critical state $s^* \in (\underline{s}, \bar{s})$ with $w_2(s) = s$ for $s \geq s^*$. That is, once (35) binds, it binds for all higher s so that workers lose insurance against fluctuations in their productivity in high states of nature. For $s < s^*$, $w_2(s)$ will again be state independent and $w_2 = w_1 \equiv \hat{w}$ if $\delta = r$. Using (33), one can show that

$$\hat{w} = \frac{1 + \varepsilon + \int_{\underline{s}}^{s^*} s \, dF(s)}{1 + F(s^*)}. \tag{36}$$

Furthermore, $\hat{w} < \bar{w}$ so that, relative to the solution with no enforcement problems, the base wage for workers is lower. It is in this way that workers pay their insurance premium for $s < s^*$. For ε small enough, (36) implies that $\hat{w} < 1$ so that workers first period wage is less than their productivity.

A model of this type is therefore able to generate the prediction of wage profiles which are steeper than productivity profiles. Wages display downward but *not* upward rigidities. In general, the slope of the wage profile reflects discount rates, interest rates and the severity of the enforcement problem through the magnitude of firm specific training (ε).

This model can be extended to generate layoffs as well if outside and inside productivities are not perfectly correlated. Holmstrom [58] does so and considers a multiperiod model with layoffs, similar to that explored in [3]. With new workers entering into the market each period and living for a finite number of years, we see that the downward rigidity of wages implies a seniority pattern for compensation. Workers with greater seniority have had more of an opportunity for their wages to be bid up by the outside markets and therefore, on average, have higher wages.

This wage structure also has implications for layoff patterns. Recall that the risk premium in Azariadis's model, $(U(w) - U(k))/U'(w)$, is an increasing function of w. From that same analysis, we found that layoff probabilities fell as the risk premium rose. Using this insight and a dynamic version of Azariadis's model, Holmstrom finds that senior workers get paid more and are laid off less than junior workers.

In sum, recognizing the importance of enforcement problems, on the workers' side of the contract, generates new implications for the contract: downward but *not* upward rigidities and seniority-layoff rules. It is possible to consider firm-enforcement problems in a similar vein. Workers will be ex post employed iff $w \leq s$: i.e. the firm will never pay insurance. For this case, the multiperiod solution will be to "bond" the firm by having it pay high wages to workers early in the contract. So, one way to deal with enforcement problems is through an appropriate structuring of intertemporal compensation to create the correct incentives for separations.

As mentioned earlier, an alternative enforcement mechanism might be reputations. While workers and/or firms might perceive short-run gains from abrogating existing contracts, this behavior might adversely affect their bargaining power in the future. A firm who fires workers in low productivity states may be unable to convince future workers that it will pay the "insurance indemnity" in low states. Hence the firm will have to offer higher average wages in the future to attract workers. As is well-known from other work on reputation models (Klein–Leffler [66], Shapiro [87] etc.) the strength of these reputation effects depends on the magnitude of discount rates, the speed by which other market participants become aware of deviations from promised behavior and the horizon of the agents. As discount rates increase, firms care less about future profits so that future losses for breach will have to be larger to enforce a contract. Similarly, to the extent that firms reputations are widely known to market participants, the gains from cheating on a contract increase as well. Finally, the horizons of firm's are important as well. In the last period of their existence, agents with finite lives will not be influenced by threats that their reputations will suffer. In some models, this may imply that reputation effects will not be present in any period.

In the labor contracts area, these reputation effects have been modeled by Bull [17], Carmichael [19], Holmstrom [57] and others. As a simple example of this approach, Carmichael considers the effects of reputations on a firm's employment behavior. A contract specifies a state-contingent compensation scheme and accedes, to the firm, the right to choose the employment level. Prospective workers have full information on a firm's past employment policies and use this information to update their forecasts of future policies.

After observing the state of nature, firms choose employment levels to maximize ex post profits plus future discounted profits. Workers' beliefs form the linkage between firms' current actions and future profits. Myopic firms have a tendency, in Carmichael's model, to overwork their current workforce. This is costly, though, as future workers will require higher compensation to work for the firm. The balance of these short-run benefits and longer term costs leads the firm to set employment inefficiently high if the firm discounts the future at all. The magnitude of this overemployment is determined by the firm's discount rate and the length of worker attachment to a given firm.

These results highlight the main point of reputations effects as an enforcement device. One can alter the process by which information is diffused throughout the economy and mapping between a firm's current actions and future constraints to develop variations on this theme. In general, though, these reputation effects never seem quite strong enough to make an implicit contract equivalent to an explicit one.[20]

As a final note, there is currently emerging an approach to the enforcement problem which focuses attention on the multilateral relationship between the courts and the contractants. Instead of taking, as given, restrictions on clauses within a contract, this approach starts by allowing fully contingent arragements between contractants. In order, though, for these arrangements to be enforceable, the court (i.e. the enforcer) must be able to observe the same variables as the worker and the firm. If there is asymmetric information present between the court and the contractants, then contracts will be incomplete.

Recent papers by Eden [26] and Hart–Moore [55] take this approach. Eden, for example, assumes that commitments to compensation payments are publicly observable but that the level of effort put forth by workers is not. Hence the firm could always claim that a worker had shirked and fire him. Eden argues that this asymmetry of information between the courts and the contractants creates an environment in which the firm, in an optimal contract, is granted the right of choosing the employment level. He then

[20] Carmichael finds that if the firm does not discount the future at all, then these outcomes coincide.

explores the implications of this additional constraint. Other variations on this theme are, of course, possible as one varies the information structure.

A summary of restricted contracts

The purpose of this section has been to explore the implications for contract design of adding a variety of restrictions to the contracting problem. The first restricted contract, following the model of Azariadis [3], generated layoffs in a setting with no worksharing and no severance pay. Under this contract, laid-off workers were worse off than their employed counterparts. Restrictions against worksharing and severance pay made agreements to share this layoff risk infeasible.

We then turned attention to the complications of asymmetric information on employment distortions. The analysis treated a variety of informational properties and their effects on employment levels. Finally, we considered the effects of other enforcement problems such as involuntary servitude and informational asymmetries between contractants and courts.

4. MACROECONOMIC IMPLICATIONS OF LABOR CONTRACTS

Thus far, we have investigated the implications of labor contracts for the allocation of labor services and risks at the level of individual firms and workers. This emphasis on the microeconomic aspects of labor contracts is in contrast to the macroeconomic motivation for the development of contracting models. This section seeks to remedy this lack of balance by concentrating on the macroeconomic implications of the contracting view of labor market behavior.

Macroeconomists tend to self-select into two groups according to their views on the flexibility of wages and prices and, as a consequence, the likelihood that the economy would be in a position of disequilibrium. One approach, often termed the fix-price model, stresses the short-run rigidity of wages and prices. Equilibrium is obtained through the use of quantity constraints on the excess demands of traders. The "auctioneer" seeks to coordinate trades by the appropriate choice of these constraints. Models of this genre have a distinct Keynesian flavor in that quantities matter more than prices in individual decision problems, inefficiencies may arise at the aggregate level and multiplier effects are possible.

Critics of this approach have argued that it lacks a "good" theory of wage and price rigidities and hence is rather ad hoc. At the time of its inception, the contracting approach was viewed as a means of understanding apparent inflexibilities in wages and prices. If successful, this would have provided a theoretical basis for the fix-price approach. With such a solid base, the model of wage-price rigidities would be a more useful device for policy evaluation since one would then be able to predict changes in wage and price setting practices in response to policy measures. We shall see that contracting models have not yet succeeded in providing a rationale for fix price models.

Besides this more theoretical motivation, as argued earlier, contracts are a feature of many market economies. What implications, if any, do these contracts have for the cyclical behavior of economies? To what extent do they influence the inflationary processes in different economies? How do they affect the conduct of stabilization policy? These are both theoretical and empirical questions. Empirically, the questions could be addressed by looking specifically at cross-section data to see whether contracting practices are correlated with central features of the business cycle. If, for example, we found that institutional differences in wage setting practices (i.e. different forms of contracts) did not produce different business cycle behavior, we might want to look elsewhere for insights into macroeconomic behavior. Theoretically, one can construct contracting models to focus directly on their implications for aggregate variables and the conduct of policy. Of course, these approaches are not mutually exclusive since the former provides some direction for the latter.

This section examines the implications of the contracting approach from both an empirical and theoretical perspective. The presentation begins with a brief discussion of contracting practices across countries. We then turn to theoretical contributions in the area of macroeconomic implications of contracts. We start with an analysis of the patterns of nominal wages. This area contains contributions which build on the microeconomic models discussed earlier and on a more macroeconomic approach to contracts. We then discuss some extensions of the models with asymmetric information to understanding macroeconomic behavior.

Empirical evidence on contracts

To begin, we consider some of the empirical evidence surrounding the issues of contract structure and macroeconomic behavior. Ideally, this evidence would take the following form. First, we would have a summary of contracting practices in a wide variety of countries including a discussion of indexation practices, contract length and some indication of the institutional features of the bargaining process. Second, we would have a summary of the prominent features of each country's macroeconomic experience in terms of key macro-variables. We could then consider what connections, if any, exist between the contracting practices and macroeconomic experiences. This search could take place at either the level of "casual" empiricism or with the use of estimation techniques.

Unfortunately, a systematic review of the macroeconomic significance of labor contracts of this type has not been completed. Instead, we must be content with descriptions of contracting practices across countries and some studies which relate these practices to specific macroeconomic variables.

Sachs [83] contains a useful summary of key contracting practices in OECD countries. In looking at his summary and other international comparisons of contracts, the U.S. and Canada stand out as exceptions in terms of the limited use of indexed agreements and in the lack of synchronized wage setting practices. In contrast, countries such as Israel, Italy and Brazil are known for their widespread use of indexation in labor contracts. Furthermore, Japan and Germany are unlike the U.S. and Canada in terms of the synchronization of wage negotiations. In Japan, most labor agreements are negotiated in a synchronized manner during the "spring wage offensive," though the contracts themselves are negotiated at the individual firm-union level. Agreements other than labor contracts often include indexing arrangements. In Israel, for example, the use of indexed financial instruments is quite widespread.

With regard to determining employment and hours per worker,

much less is known. For the most part, contracts seem to be quite specific about compensation rules and much less specific about employment patterns. Hence, we have little information on the details of employment practices across contracts. However, there are a few regularities across countries worth noting.

Japan, with its system of permanent employment, is known for its infrequent use of layoffs as a means of reducing total hours. Instead, worksharing is very prominent though layoffs apparently do occur in the face of permanent shocks (e.g. the oil shock in the 1970s). For the U.S., in contrast, worksharing seems much less prominent and temporary layoffs more widespread. Differences in the form of employment variations across countries can perhaps partially be attributed to differences in unemployment insurance schemes. See Gordon [39] for a discussion of employment differences in the U.K., U.S. and Japan.

In light of this heterogeneity in contracting practices, what differences do we observe in the macroeconomic performances of these countries? First, with regard to average rates of inflation, it is quite clear that the countries displaying large degrees of indexation (e.g. Israel and Brazil) are also countries which have experienced periods of severe inflation. To the extent that higher inflation rates and larger errors in forecasting inflation come hand in hand, one could argue that the observed differences in indexation are a consequence of higher inflation rates. Alternatively, it might be that because of the predominance of indexation clauses in individual agreements, governments feel much less need to pursue anti-inflation policies. Hence, we have an apparent correlation between indexation and average inflation rates but no clear causality. For the U.S. and Canada, the percentage of contracts including cost of living clauses has varied over time and appears to be correlated with the inflation rate as well.[21]

As stated earlier, contracts generally do not contain clauses specifying employment schedules in the manner suggested by the theoretical models discussed earlier. Hence it is difficult to obtain direct evidence on any relationship between patterns of indexation and employment variations. We can consider this as a situation in which the firm is granted discretion in the choice of employment.

---

[21] See Dornbusch–Simonsen [25] for an elaborate discussion of indexation issues.

This choice is constrained by the compensation made explicit in the contract and by any reputation effects that may link the firm's selection with future costs of attracting workers. To the extent that these reputation effects are unimportant, the firm's choice of employment will be to select a point on the labor demand curve. To the extent that fluctuations are driven by demand shocks, we would expect to see evidence of counter-cyclical real wages when looking at contracts which do not contain full indexation (such as those in the U.S. and Canada).

Geary–Kennan [36] is one of many studies which investigate the cyclical pattern of real wages. From their research, they could not reject the view that employment and real wages were independent. This is consistent with the theoretical result obtained earlier that wages and employment are set independently. This type of result is also consistent with the view expressed by Hall [47] that wage payments in a given period represent installment payments on the purchase of labor services over long periods of time (the discussion on enforcement brings out this view of long term contracts as well). These results, of course, shed some doubt on models (some of which are discussed below) which view employment as being demand-determined.

In related work, Gordon [39], Sachs [83] and Branson–Rotemberg [15] compare wage-setting practices and business cycle behavior between the U.S., Europe and Japan. The consensus view seems to be that the U.S. displays more nominal wage rigidity than the others. Sachs and Branson–Rotemberg further argue that both Europe and Japan display more real wage rigidity than the U.S. From this, Sachs argues that the prolonged experience of high unemployment in Europe is due to this real wage rigidity.

In short, there does not appear to be compelling evidence that the differences in contracting practices manifest themselves, on a one-for-one basis, with particular features of business cycles in these countries.[22] We will return to these issues once again in the discussion of macroeconomic implications of contracting models.

[22] One possible approach would be to do a "contracts version" of Lucas [69] and investigate correlations between indexation parameters and the response of output to money shocks. See Fethke [30] for work in this direction.

Macro-contracting models

To begin our discussion of the theoretical implications of contracts at the macro-level, we consider an approach which does not rest firmly on the microeconomic theory presented earlier. Nonetheless, papers in this area do provide some useful insights into the macroeconomic implications of contracting and the role of monetary policy in such an economy. We will return to consider the microfoundations of these contracting models in the next subsection.

This research on macro-contracting models was apparently begun in response to the strong results obtained by Lucas [68, 69] and Sargent–Wallace [86] and others on the neutrality of anticipated monetary policy. Fischer [32] and Phelps–Taylor [76] described situations in which these neutrality results may not arise once market-clearing is no longer assumed. This approach was thus meant to resurrect monetary policy as an effective policy measure.

The approach taken by Fischer [32] was to describe the operation of the labor markets quite differently than Lucas [68, 69] and Sargent–Wallace [86]. In particular, Fischer assumes that labor services are traded through contracts of a very special nature. Contracts are negotiated for T periods and specify nominal wages to apply for each of these periods. The level of employment is assumed to be determined by the firm after it observes all relevant information. Hence, in comparison to the contracts described earlier, these arrangements simply specify a nominal wage for each period and grant the firm the right to choose employment. Fischer then investigates the rational expectations equilibrium for this type of model.

Stated formally, Fischer's model contains three equations: (all variables are in logs).

$$Y_t^s = \alpha + 1/L \sum_{i=1}^{L} (P_t - {}_{t-i}W_t) + u_t \tag{37}$$

$$Y_t^D = M_t - P_t + v_t, \tag{38}$$

and

$${}_{t-i}W_t = {}_{t-i}P_t. \tag{39}$$

The first equation is an aggregate supply relation expressing output as a function of a technological variable (α) and technology (real) shock u_t and a weighted average of real wages. The variable L is the length of the average contract. At any point in time, $1/L$ of the firms are in period $i = 1, 2, \ldots, L$ of their contract. A contract negotiated i periods ago specifies a nominal wage $({}_{t-i}W_t)$ to apply in period t. The firm is given the latitude to choose employment given this wage structure after observing the price level P_t. The second equation is an expression for aggregate demand with a (nominal) shock v_t. The third equation represents wage setting in the model as workers and firms attempt to stabilize the worker's real wage. Contracts negotiated in period i set the wage in period $t({}_{t-i}W_t)$ equal to (the log of) the price which is expected to prevail in period $t({}_{t-i}P_t)$.

Fischer also assumes that the shocks follow first-order autoregressive schemes so that

$$u_t = \rho_1 u_{t-1} + \varepsilon_t \quad 0 < \rho_1 < 1$$

and

$$v_t = \rho_2 v_{t-1} + \eta_t \quad 0 < \rho_2 < 1,$$

where ε_t and η_t are simply white noise terms. Finally, Fischer stipulates that the monetary authorities follow a rule in which the money stock depends solely on previous shocks, i.e.

$$M_t = \sum_{i=1}^{\infty} a_i u_{t-i} + \sum_{i=1}^{\infty} b_i v_{t-i}. \tag{40}$$

The usual method for solving rational expectations models is then employed. That is, one solves for the price level as a function of price expectations and then uses the assumption of rational expectations to close the model.

The rational expectations solution will clearly depend on the average contract length term, L. Fischer first assumes that $L = 1$ so that all agents sign 1-year contracts *prior* to the determination of u_t and v_t but with full information on the values of past shocks. In this equilibrium, output is indpendent of the parameters of the money supply rule. So, as in the market clearing models such as [86], changes in the monetary authority's feedback rule would have no real effects.

Fischer then considers the behavior of the economy when $L = 2$. In any time period, half of the contracts are one year old and the other half have just been negotiated. Solving for the rational expectations equilibrium,

$$y_t = \tfrac{1}{2}(\varepsilon_t - \eta_t) + \tfrac{1}{3}[\varepsilon_{t-1}(a_1 + 2\rho_1) + \eta_{t-1}(b_1 - \rho_2)] + \rho_1^2 u_{t-2}. \quad (41)$$

Hence, in contrast to the model with one-period contracts, the parameters of (40) have effects on real output. For $L = 2$, the parameters for u_{t-1} and v_{t-1} (a_1 and b_1) matter for determining output in period 2. If we were to allow L to increase, then more terms of the feedback rule would appear in (41).

Agents in this economy are not fooled by money injections as they are in Lucas [68, 69] and Sargent–Wallace [86]. Instead contracts have an element of predetermination which allows the authorities to act more quickly in light of current information. The contractants realize that the authorities will have this added flexibility, but cannot (given the restrictions placed on the contracts) offset this advantage. That is, the contractants would (if permitted) index their wages to past values of (ε_t, η_t) which would restore the neutrality results. Fischer argues that generally these indexed contracts will be too complicated and too costly to implement so that we usually observe the simple contracts with predetermined nominal wages as used in his model.

The work by Gray [40] represents a further application of this macro-contracting approach. Gray considers a model in which indexation of the nominal wage to the price level is feasible. In the model there are real shocks to the firm's technology and nominal shocks which affect the money supply. Contracts are one-period agreements which stipulate a base money wage, an indexation parameter and, as in Fischer's model, grant to the firm the right to choose employment ex post. Assuming that the base wage is set so that the labor market would clear if all disturbances were at their mean values, Gray's analysis focuses on the choice of the degree of indexation in the contract.

To model this choice, Gray assumes that the indexation parameter is set to minimize variations in output around the value it would obtain if labor was traded in a spot market. This level of output, of course, reflects realizations of the real random variable but is independent of the nominal disturbance. Gray shows that if all shocks to the system were nominal, the optimal degree of indexation would be one. If, alternatively, only real shocks were present, the optimal degree of indexation would be strictly between zero and one so that employment would vary with the real shock. When both shocks are present, the optimal degree of indexation is a convex combination of these two extremes. Increases in the relative variance of the nominal (real) shock tend to increase (decrease) the optimal degree of indexation. Gray uses these results to point out that the optimal degree of indexation is generally less than unity so that policies which advocate full indexation may be suboptimal.[23]

Gray [41] extends this approach to focus on the joint determination of contract length and indexation. Her model extends the framework outlined above by allowing the shocks to technology and the money supply to follow a Weiner process. Hence, forecast variances increase with time. Gray also assumes that there are costs of negotiation each time a new contract is established.

The optimal degree of indexation is characterized by the same type of tradeoff discussed in her earlier paper. The gains to longer contracts come from spreading out the fixed cost of negotiation over longer periods of time. Long-term contracts are costly, though, since the forecast variance of the shock increases over time. Hence, contract terms are more likely to lead to large deviations between actual and desired employment levels over time. The optimal contract length balances these gains and losses. For a given degree of indexation, contract length therefore decreases as the variability of the shocks increases. Gray also demonstrates that if indexation is costly, we would observe some short term non-indexed contracts and some longer term contracts with indexation provisions. Increases in the variance of the money shock would lead to more indexation in contracts.

Taylor [91] and Gertler [37] have focused on the time series properties of macro-contracting models. Taylor considers a model with staggered contracts so that only a fraction of all agreements are being negotiated at a point in time. Contractants, in Taylor's model, are concerned with their relative wage position and hence look at contracts negotiated previously and those to be negotiated in the future before deciding on their compensation level. Taylor assumes that compensation is predetermined for the length of the contract and that the firm chooses the employment level, ex post. The main

[23] Also see Fischer [33].

contribution of this approach is that the model reproduces certain time series properties of the U.S. economy—in particular correlated movements in output and employment which exceed the length of most contracts. This approach, if one accepts the relative wage hypothesis, thus adds a considerable amount of persistence to output and employment variations in these models.

Gertler [37] considers a learning procedure in the basic Fischer model. Contracts are one-period in nature but agents are unable to discriminate between temporary and permanent shocks. Their learning behavior creates correlations in output and employment.

In many ways, the approach taken in these, and related papers, to understanding the implications of contracts for macroeconomic behavior is quite compelling. The results are relatively intuitive and clean. The approach seems capable of generating predictions that link up with certain empirical evidence (at least for the U.S.). For macroeconomists, this class of models has provided a useful starting point for focusing on other implications of contracts.

There has, however, been some criticism of this approach based largely on the specification of the contracts. Barro [9] argued that the employment rule (giving the firm the right to choose employment) assumed in these models left ex post gains to trade unexploited and hence represented an inefficiency in the contract which required an explanation. As discussed further in the next section, the contracts used in these papers are not derived directly from optimization problems. Therefore, the employment rules specified and the compensation schemes used do not necessarily match the schedules that would be generated by an optimal labor contract.

From that perspective, it is not clear that this class of models has advanced our understanding of wage/price rigidities very much beyond the insights of the fix-price literature. By assuming a contractural structure instead of generating it from optimizing behavior, these models are subject to the same criticisms as fix-price models. Why are wages non-responsive to economic events? Why are quantities set in a sub-optimal fashion?

One defense of this approach, often heard, is that real world contracts match those assumed in the framework outlined above. That is, most contracts say very little about employment levels but instead allow the firm to choose this variable ex post. As argued earlier, whether or not this implies that the employment level is on the labor demand curve depends on the strength of the reputation effect and other considerations. Furthermore, the empirical evidence by Geary–Kennan and others leads to some doubt about the strong prediction of these models that the real wage should be countercyclical when fluctuations are caused by demand shocks.

In sum, there is a large body of research focusing attention on the macroeconomic consequences of labor contracts. The methods used in this approach seem to shed little light on the factors determining the overall structure of contracts and instead focus on the consequences of some prespecified forms of contracts. To the extent that these contracting practices are not independent of government policies, this approach can lead to misleading results on the effects of policies. Hence, doing policy evaluation with these models, or other types of comparative statics, may be misleading.[24]

Macroeconomic implications of optimal labor contracts

As pointed out above, the macro-contracting models focus on the consequences of specific contracting structures without providing any firm justification for them. The obvious remedy for this state of affairs is to develop the microeconomic base for macro-contracting models. The point of this section is to illustrate some of the possible macro-implications of *optimal* labor contracts as well as some of the difficulties with providing these micro-foundations.

The optimal contracts literature, as explored earlier, characterizes state-contingent compensation levels and, independently, state-contingent employment levels. As was emphasized, the employment rule need not correspond to points on either the labor supply or labor demand curves. This is in sharp contrast to the assumptions made in the macro-contracting models that employment is demand determined. This is also not the same as the rationing assumptions made in the fix-price literature. Hence, in terms of employment rules, the optimal contracts literature does not support the assumptions used in either of these approaches. This was, of course, Barro's [9] point.

[24] See Fethke–Policano [31] for an example of this which endogenizes the timing of contract renegotiations.

What about compensation schemes? It is possible to find microeconomic foundations to support the compensation system assumed in the macro-contracting models?

By placing the optimal labor contracts problem into a more elaborate dynamic model with money, we can begin to address these questions. Suppose, to start, that changes in the money supply are immediately observed by all agents in some economy. As optimizing agents, workers and firms would completely index compensation to the money shocks thus leaving real compensation and employment independent of the money supply. Consequently, money injections are completely neutral and this contracting model would provide no insights on the (supposed) correlations between money and output.

Of course, the models by Fischer, Gray and Taylor prohibited this type of direct indexation of compensation to the money stock. Fischer and Taylor assumed that money wages were predetermined (though not necessarily constant) over the life of the contract. Gray allowed for indexation through the choice of a parameter determining the sensitivity of wages to prices. From a microeconomic perspective, it is useful to consider the possible causes of this incomplete indexation.

One conceivable cause of imperfect indexation is incomplete information. Suppose the economy is subject to a variety of real and nominal shocks, both transitory and permanent. As in Lucas [68], one can imagine a situation in which observations on prices and other signals are not sufficient to enable market participants to completely determine the state of the world. Forward-looking agents need to extract information on the value of permanent shocks from their current observations in order to forecast future prices. To the extent that the observables are not fully revealing of the underlying shocks, a signal extraction problem arises. Contracting models with this feature have been explored by Azariadis [4] and Cooper [23] and an example of this approach is given below.

Consider an overlapping generations structure in which an equal number (θ) of risk neutral and risk averse agents are born each period. The risk neutral agents are endowed with a technology for converting labor (l) into output (y) with a production function given by $y = f(l)$. We assume that $f(\cdot)$ is strictly increasing and concave. The risk averse agents are endowed with a unit divisible leisure time which they will supply to the firms in return for a money wage, w.

Both types of agents are involved in production in youth and both consume only in old age. Hence the allocative decision here is the level of employment, *not* savings. Money is the sole store of value in this economy.

The uncertainty in the model is a consequence of both real and nominal shocks to the system as in Lucas [68]. In particular, suppose that the aggregate money supply in period t is given by

$$m_t = m_{t-1}\tilde{x}_t$$

when $\tilde{x}_t$ is a random variable and m_{t-1} is the money supply from the previous period. The random money creations (through different realizations of $\tilde{x}_t$) are distributed in proportion to existing money holdings so that the distribution of wealth is not influenced directly. We assume that realizations of $\tilde{x}_t$ are uncorrelated across time.

The real shock can be simply modeled by assuming that the aggregate number of worker-firm pairs active at a point in time (θ_t) is random. Further, suppose that $\tilde{\theta}_t$ is a serially uncorrelated random variable. If this was a multi-sector economy as in Lucas [68], $\tilde{\theta}_t$ could represent the number of worker-firm pairs that decide to reside and produce in a particular sector. One could then take results for one sector to provide insights into aggregate behavior. We take the simpler route here and view $\tilde{\theta}_t$ as an aggregate real shock. This modelling of real uncertainty is simply a way to capture real shocks to the economy *without* creating situations of asymmetric information between workers and firms.

The information structure of the model is quite simple. Young agents (workers and firms) observe aggregate prices but do not observe $\tilde{x}_t$ and $\tilde{\theta}_t$ independently. Old agents observe their money transfer but do not (cannot) provide this information to the young agents. This imperfect information provides the rationale for indexing wages to current prices but not to underlying disturbances.

In this economy, the consumption of a worker born in period t is

$$c_{t+1}^w = \frac{w_t x_{t+1}}{P_{t+1}}$$

where w_t is the nominal compensation paid by the firm, x_{t+1} is the random money transfer and P_{t+1} is the random price in the worker's old age (the time of consumption). We represent worker's preferences over consumption and labor (l_t) by $u(c_{t+1}^w) - g(l_t)$ where

$u' > 0$, $u'' < 0$, $g' > 0$, $g'' > 0$. The firm's consumption is given by

$$c^f_{t+1} = \frac{(P_t f(l_t) - w_t)x_{t+1}}{P_{t+1}}$$

since $P_t f(l_t) - w_t$ is the firm's nominal profits in earned youth.

The reader familiar with Lucas [68] or Azariadis [5] will notice the parallels between the models. Those models treated the worker-firm pair as perfectly integrated and ignored risk sharing. In the contracting case, we are interested in the split of the proceeds from production between the worker and the firm through the specification of nominal wages contingent on prices.

A labor contract between a worker-firm pair in period t specifies compensation $w(P_t)$ and hours worked $l(P_t)$ as functions of the observable output price P_t. Note that we have assumed work in period t must be paid for in that period. Hence, contracts are stipulated in nominal terms. Letting λ represent a bargaining weight for an arbitrary worker-firm pair (we don't have ex ante markets here to pin down the equilibrium otherwise), the optimal contract

$$\text{maximizes } E\{u(c^w_{t+1}) - g(l(P_t)) + \lambda c^F_{t+1}\}.$$

Here the expectation is taken with respect to P_t, x_{t+1} and P_{t+1} since the contract is negotiated before P_t is known and (c^w_{t+1}, c^f_{t+1}) are defined above.

The optimal contract satisfies

$$\frac{g'(l_t)}{f'(l_t)} \equiv H(l_t) = \lambda E\left[\frac{P_t x_{t+1}}{P_{t+1}} \,\middle|\, P_t\right], \tag{42}$$

and

$$E\left[\frac{w_t x_{t+1}}{P_{t+1}} u'\left(\frac{w_t x_{t+1}}{P_{t+1}}\right) \,\middle|\, P_t\right] = \lambda E\left[\frac{w_t x_{t+1}}{P_{t+1}} \,\middle|\, P_t\right] \quad \text{for all } P_t. \tag{43}$$

Given our assumptions on $g(\cdot)$ and $f(\cdot)$, $H(l_t)$ is strictly increasing.

Following Lucas [68], one can use the market clearing conditions along with a conjecture on prices and these two conditions on the optimal contract to fully characterize a rational expectations equilibrium for this type of an economy. That exercise would take us too far afield and we will simply assume that an equilibrium exists and focus on the properties of $w(P_t)$ and $l(P_t)$ in such an equilibrium.[25]

The key to the analysis is the conditioning of expectations on P_t in the two first-order conditions. In particular, what information about x_{t+1}/P_{t+1} is contained in observations of P_t? Suppose, for example, that shocks to x_t were not present. Then, current observations on P_t would not provide information on P_{t+1} since θ_{t+1} is, by assumption, independent of θ_t. So, from (42), l_t would be an increasing function of P_t since $H'(\cdot)>0$ by assumption. At the other extreme, if $\tilde{\theta}_t$ is not random, then there is an equilibrium in which shocks to P_t are transmitted proportionately to P_{t+1}. In this case, the expected real return to work conditional on P_t (the right side of (42)) is constant. Money is therefore neutral.

In the presence of imperfect information about (x_t, θ_t), agents recognize that high values of P_t can be due to either large injections of money (high x_t) or a relatively small number of traders (low θ_t). The contractants don't observe (x_t, θ_t) directly and must infer something about these variables from P_t. Observing large P_t leads agents to place more probability weight on low values of θ_t and high values of x_t. Hence, as P_t increases, agents expect that next period's price will be large too so $E[x_{t+1}/P_{t+1} \mid P_t]$ decreases with P_t. However, agents also realize that a large P_t could be due to a low θ_t which would have no influence on P_{t+1}. On balance, $E[(P_t x_{t+1}/P_{t+1}) \mid P_t]$ may increase with P_t and we will assume that it does.[26]

With this (implicit) restriction on the distributions in mind, (42) implies that employment increases with P_t since $H'(\cdot)>0$. As in Lucas [68], changes in the money supply (via $\tilde{x}_t$) create variations in employment because agents conjecture that price increases are partly due to real factors (low $\tilde{\theta}_t$). The responsiveness of hours to variations in P_t depend critically on the responsiveness of the

[25] Market clearing for this economy requires $P_t Y_t \theta_t = m_{t-1} X_t$. Note that because *all* agents consume only in old age, the nominal demand for goods in period t is simply the money supply and is independent of the wage schedule. Since $y_t = f(l_t)$ and the employment rule given in (42) is independent of w_t, we can use (42) and market clearing to determine the output and price functions for the economy. Using these (43) will characterize the compensation schedule. Hence the model is quite similar to Lucas [68] and the existence proof provided there should be applicable here as well.

[26] See Lucas [68] for a precise statement of these conditions.

conditional expectation of P_t/P_{t+1} variations in P_t and on the curvature of $H(l_t)$.

With regard to compensation patterns, (41) is the appropriate condition for efficient risk sharing given that agents observe P_t and try to forecast (x_{t+1}, P_{t+1}). The sensitivity of compensation to prices depends, again, on the sensitivity of $E(1/P_{t+1})$ to movements in P_t *and* on the properties of workers' preferences. Let $v(c^w_{t+1}) \equiv c^w_{t+1}u'(c^w_{t+1})$ so that (43) is simply

$$E[v(c^w_{t+1}) \mid P_t] = \lambda E\left[\frac{w_t x_{t+1}}{P_{t+1}} \middle| P_t\right].$$

The sign of v' depends on the workers' degree of risk aversion. That is

$$v'(c^w_{t+1}) = c^w_{t+1}u''(c^w_{t+1}) + u'(c^w_{t+1}) = u'(c^w_{t+1})(1 - R(c^w_{t+1}))$$

where $R(c^w_{t+1})$ is the workers' relative degree of risk aversion. If $R(c^w_{t+1}) \equiv 1$ for all c^w_{t+1}, then the left-hand side of (41) is independent of P_t and $w(P_t)$ is determined so that $E[w(P_t)x_{t+1}/P_{t+1} \mid P_t]$ is constant as P_t varies. Hence $w(P_t)$ is an increasing function. If $R(\cdot) > 1$, then $v' > 0$ and again $w(P_t)$ is an increasing function. When $R(\cdot) < 1$, it is possible that $w(P_t)$ is actually a decreasing function.

In the extreme case of no real shocks to the economy, the optimal contract would fully index $w(P_t)$ since observations on P_t reveal $\tilde{x}_t$. This holds for all specifications of workers' preferences. If, alternatively, the distribution of $\tilde{x}_t$ was degenerate, the optimal contract would set $w(P_t)$ independently of P_t as a form of optimal insurance. When both shocks are present, the optimal degree of indexation will reflect the information that P_t conveys about P_{t+1}.

In many ways, this model can provide some support for the macro-contracting models of Gray. If changes in the relative variances of the shocks influence these conditional expectations in the expected way—i.e. as the variability of $\tilde{\theta}$ increases relative to that of $\tilde{x}$, observations on P_t should provide less information on P_{t+1}—then the sensitivity of wages to prices will reflect these relative variances as Gray suggests. If the variability of $\tilde{x}_t$ is relatively low and there are costs of indexing compensation, then, as Fischer assumes, the optimal contract may simply specify a predetermined level of compensation (though not necessarily a fixed nominal wage).

To what extent does the contracting approach provide insights into fluctuations in money and output and the conduct of monetary policy which differ from the predictions of the "market-clearing" models of Lucas, Sargent–Wallace and others? Expression (42) which determines the pattern of employment variations as prices vary could have been obtained from a version of Lucas' [68] model.[27] In that sense, this model and that of Lucas [68] are observationally equivalent.

Does the contracting model generate different results with regard to the conduct of monetary policy? Here the answer is maybe. As pointed out in Azariadis [5], in a variant of the model in Lucas [68], changes in the monetary policy rule which influence the amount of information conveyed by the price system will not be neutral even if this policy change is known by all agents. Polemarchakis–Weiss [78] and Azariadis [5] also point out that deterministic monetary policy may not be optimal in these models. While a deterministic monetary policy may clarify price signals, this policy doesn't shield agents from real shocks.

As suggested in Cooper [23] for a model similar to the one explored here, the presence of labor contracts as a source of insurance may alter this result on optimal policy. By stabilizing the monetary shock, the real shock is revealed through the price level. Hence private insurance arrangements (such as labor contracts) may be able to shield agents from the risks that remain in the absence of monetary disturbances. That is, the conduct of monetary policy can influence the completeness of the existing set of markets. So, macroeconomic contracting models may have different policy implications than the market clearing models with imperfect information.

In sum, the optimal contracting approach can be extended to a macro-economic setting with real and nominal shocks. Some support for the compensation patterns in Fischer [32] and Gray [40] can be provided. Nonetheless, there seems to be little theoretical support for the employment rules assumed in those models.

---

[27] Suppose, in the model, young agents had preferences specified by $c_{t+1} - g(h_t)$ and that the technology was $f(h_t) = y_t$. Then, with $c_{t+1} = P_t y_t x_{t+1}/P_{t+1}$, (42) would characterize the labor supply decision of a young agent.

Aggregate implications of asymmetric information contracting models

In addition to extending the optimal contracts model to focus on nominal compensation patterns, it is also possible (and interesting) to obtain some macroeconomic implications from the models of asymmetric information. This section briefly discusses two such attempts.

Grossman, Hart and Maskin [46] consider the aggregate implications of the models developed in [44, 45] and discussed in the previous section. Suppose that the economy consists of many worker-firm pairs in which firms are risk averse and workers are risk neutral. Employment and compensation are determined in an optimal labor contract. Grossman, Hart and Maskin consider a setting in which both aggregate and firm-specific (idiosyncratic) shocks exist. Workers have imperfect information about the shocks affecting their own productivity but are perfectly informed about aggregate shocks. These informational assumptions are in contrast to those employed by Lucas [68, 69] in which local, but not aggregate, information was readily available.

Variations in aggregate variables can then influence the magnitudes of the distortions at the worker-firm level by affecting the information set of the contractants. As an extreme example of this, Grossman, Hart and Maskin suppose that the aggregate shock takes on one of the two values: n_1 and n_2. When n_1 occurs, workers are fully informed about their own productivities while if n_2 occurs they are not. As a consequence, even if the shocks to worker productivity at the firm level are totally idiosyncratic, aggregate employment will be lower when n_2 occurs due to the presence of the asymmetric information.

To illustrate this point further, Grossman, Hart and Maskin create a simple general equilibrium model in which workers are employed by producers of intermediate products. Final goods producers combine intermediate products and sell their output to customers. These producers have stochastic technologies and face random demand curves. Hence, the demand functions for intermediate goods reflect both sources of uncertainty. Workers, as consumers, may be informed about demand for final goods by observing relative prices but may still be uninformed about the demand for the product they help to produce. Hence, we again have a situation of asymmetric information and employment distortions.

One of the gains from placing this type of contracting problem in a general equilibrium setting is that spillover effects across worker-firm pairs can be analyzed. Demand shocks (brought about by random endowments) change relative prices of final goods in the economy. The intermediate goods producers experience fluctuations in the value of their products and, for the unfortunate ones, unemployment results as part of the optimal labor contract. In equilibrium, though, these inefficient layoffs create reductions in employment in *other sectors* of the economy. Thus, the low levels of employment in one sector (due to the design of optimal labor contracts) creates a tendency towards lower levels of output and employment economy-wide.

Farmer [27, 28] extends the contracting model with asymmetric information to obtain some interesting implications concerning the interaction of interest rates, layoffs and bankruptcies. In most of the contracting models discussed thus far, the worker-firm pair determined a contract ex ante taking into account the other opportunities they may have had at the time of negotiation. As in most models of risk-sharing arrangements though, there is always the possibility that bankruptcy or limited liability conditions (i.e. ex post contraints on levels of income) can alter the formulation of these contracts. Drawing on the related research of Sappington [84], Farmer investigates the macroeconomic implications of limited liability constraints.

To understand this point, consider a basic principal-agent model, in which both of these individuals are risk neutral. One can then resolve any incentives problem created by the principal's inability to completely monitor the agent's actions by asking the agent to pay a fixed amount to the principal. The agent bears all of the risk and, as the "owner" of the project, is induced to take an efficient action. Sappington pointed out that if the agent's liability is limited so that he/she is unable to make the required payments to the principal in each state, then this scheme will not resolve the incentive problem. The presence of limited liability essentially creates risk averse behavior by an otherwise risk neutral agent.

Farmer [27, 28] applies this type of result to the contracting models. Suppose that both workers and firms are risk neutral and the firm faces a bankruptcy constraint in that its profits cannot fall beneath a minimal level, $\bar{\Pi}$. This level, $\bar{\Pi}$, could be interpreted as the firm's ex post opportunity or part of a cash-flow constraint. In the presence of asymmetric information about workers' productivity at the firm, Farmer shows that the bankruptcy constraint can (if it is binding) create employment distortions analogous to those described in Proposition 4 since these constraints create risk averse behavior by the firm.

Macroeconomic conditions can then influence the likelihood of unemployment by affecting the probability that this bankruptcy constraint binds. Farmer [27, 28] shows that increases in interest rates can increase the probability of bankruptcy and unemployment when firms are parties to both loan contracts and labor contracts. As interest rates increase, the average profits of a firm fall (since it is more costly to finance its capital acquisitions) so that the bankruptcy constraint is more likely to bind. These theoretical predictions can then be related to the empirical work in [67].

Summary

This section has illustrated some of the insights the contracting approach has for understanding macroeconomic behavior. It is well understood, that money non-neutralities can be generated by models which exhibit some wage/price rigidities or in models which assume agents are unable to distinguish real and nominal shocks. What then has the existing contracting literature added to our understanding of this phenomena?

The answer, at this stage, seems to be "very little". The first class of contracting models discussed in this section are really reincarnations of fix-price models. They assert particular compensation schemes (Gray [40] is an exception) and rely on inefficient schemes for determing quantities. These models are therefore subject to the same criticisms that have hampered fix-price models.

The second class of models were not subject to this criticism as the contracts were generated by optimizing behavior. Nonetheless, the mechanism by which money influenced real activity was identical to that originally proposed by Lucas [68]. So the presence of contracts did not create a new avenue for monetary influences. Rather, the model simply helped illuminate the effects of money on nominal wages and employment levels.

The models of asymmetric information did have some interesting macroeconomic consequences. Yet, at this early stage, their ability to help in understanding correlations between real and nominal variables is not clear.

5. SUMMARY AND CONCLUSIONS

The contracts literature began as an attempt to understand the existence of fairly large fluctuations in output and employment without corresponding fluctuations in wages. In contrast to the view that wages decentralize employment decisions by balancing supplies and demand, the contracting approach emphasizes that wages serve as instruments for a provision of insurance and credit between the worker and the firm. Employment is determined either through explicit agreement or at the firm's discretion with the "reputation effect" acting to limit this power. This separation of wages from the determination of employment represents a radical departure from the traditional views on decentralization.

What are the gains from this departure? This survey has illustrated some of these through an analysis of microeconomic relations between workers and firms and their macroeconomic implications. Besides discussing the independent role of wages, we focused on the distortions created by the presence of asymmetric information and enforcement problems. In this way, the contracts literature provided implications which diverge from the complete contingents markets models of Arrow and Debreu. The last section addressed the implications of labor contracts for business cycles behavior. With perfect information and costless indexation, the presence of contracts has no impact on fluctuations in output and employment. Hence, as Barro [9] suggested, the presence of contracts, per se, need not create any macroeconomic inefficiencies or fluctuations not present in market clearing models. However, once we introduce asymmetries in information and/or other types of transactions costs, the contracting approach make a difference.

What are the weaknesses of this approach and what developments in this area can we foresee? Presumably these two issues are related in that future research will seek to address these weaknesses.

First, one is struck by the limited amount of empirical evidence (at either the micro-or-macro level) which guides research in this area. The theoretical results on the design of contracts simply swamp the evidence available on them. To some, this is an important weakness which will (one hopes) stimulate further empirical work in this area and the derivation of theoretical models which contain clear testable implications.

Second, the contracting approach has yet to yield a robust explanation of underemployment and distortions in employment relations. The results presented in Section III suffer from their extreme sensitivity to the underlying specification of preferences. Furthermore, with the exceptions of Grossman, Hart and Maskin [46] and Farmer [27, 28], we have little evidence that the contracting approach can deliver useful predictions for macroeconomic variables. This is particularly true for understanding correlations between real and nominal variables.

One possible remedy for this is to imbed contracts into a general equilibrium setting. As suggested by the work of Hosios [59], the interaction of contractural terms and aggregate variables may yield interesting macroeconomic insights. Further, Weitzman's [93] work on the macroeconomic consequences of alternative compensation schemes highlights a potentially interesting externality between privately negotiated contracts and aggregate economic behavior. Both of these papers and others in this area share an important theme: the terms of individual contracts depend on aggregate variables. This feedback relationship has the potential of generating interesting coordination failures.

Another approach is to explicitly model the interaction of contracts in labor, product and credit markets. Perhaps nominal rigidities emerge in labor contracts because of their presence in other contracts. The credit market models have the added benefit of modeling a more interesting channel for the influence of money when compared to the common assumption of proportional transfers.

Whether or not the contracting approach will eventually contain the key to understanding (and influencing) business cycles remains an open question. The goal of this monograph has been more modest: to provide an overview of the implicit contracting models' accomplishments and weaknesses as a means of stimulating further research in this intriguing area of economics.

References

References marked with a single asterisk denote works essential to an understanding of the field, to which the reader should turn first for a deeper knowledge of the topics covered in this survey. Those marked with a double asterisk are mentioned in the text but not so basic to the field. All the references listed are mentioned at some point in the text of this survey.

[1] Akerlof, G. and H. Miyazaki, "The Wage Bill Agrument Meets the Implicit Contract Theory of Unemployment," *Review of Economic Studies,* **47 (1980), 321–338.

[2] Arrow, K. J., "The Role of Securities in the Optimal Allocation of Risk Bearing," *Review of Economic Studies,* **31 (1964), 91–96.

*[3] Azariadis, C., "Implicit Contracts and Underemployment Equilibria," *Journal of Political Economy,* **83** (1975), 1183–1202.

*[4] Azariadis, C., "Escalator Clauses and the Allocation of Cyclical Risks," *Journal of Economic Theory,* **18** (1978), 119–155.

[5] Azariadis, C., "A Reexamination of Natural Rate Theory," *American Economic Review,* **71 (1981), 946–960.

*[6] Azariadis, C., "Implicit Contracts and Related Topics: A Survey," in *The Economics of the Labour Market* ed. by Z. Hornstein, *et al.* London: HMSO, 1981.

*[7] Azariadis, C., "Employment with Asymmetric Information," *Quarterly Journal of Economics* (Supplement), **98** (1983), 157–173.

*[8] Baily, M. N., "Wages and Employment Under Uncertain Demand," *Review of Economic Studies,* **41** (1974), 37–50.

*[9] Barro, R. J., "Long-term Contracting, Sticky Prices and Monetary Policy," *Journal of Monetary Economics,* **3** (1977), 305–316.

[10] Barro, R. J. and H. J. Grossman, "A General Disequilibrium Model of Income and Employment," *American Economic Review,* **61 (1971), 82–93.

**[11] Becker, G. S., *Human Capital.* New York: Columbia University Press, 1964.

[12] Benassy, J. P., "Neo-Keynesian Disequilibrium in a Monetary Economy," *Review of Economic Studies,* **42** (1975), 502–523.

[13] Blanchard, O., "Wage Indexing Rules and the Behavior of the Economy," *Journal of Political Economy,* **87** (1979), 798–815.

*[14] Borch, K., "Equilibrium in a Reinsurance Market," *Econometrica,* **30** (1962), 424–444.

[15] Branson, W. and J. Rotenberg., "International Adjustment with Wage Rigidity," *European Economic Review,* **13 (1980), 309–332.

[16] Brown, M. and E. Wolfstetter., "Underemployment and Normal Leisure," *Economic Letters,* **15** (1984), 157–163.

*[17] Bull, C., "The Existence of Self-Enforcing Implicit Contracts," C. V. Starr Center, New York University, 1983.

[18] Calvo, G. and E. Phelps, "Employment Contingent Wage Contracts," *Journal of Monetary Economics,* **5 (1977), 160–168.

*[19] Carmichael, L., "Reputations in the Labor Market," *American Economic Review,* **74** (1984), 713–725.

*[20] Chari, V. V., "Involuntary Unemployment and Implicit Contracts," *Quarterly Journal of Economics* (Supplement), **98** (1983), 107–122.

*[21] Cooper, R., "A Note on Overemployment/Underemployment in Labor Contracts Under Asymmetric Information, *Economic Letters,* **12** (1983), 81–87.

*[22] Cooper, R., "Worker Asymmetric Information and Employment Distortions," *Journal of Labor Economics,* **3** (1985), 188–208.
**[23] Cooper, R., "Optimal Labor Contracts and the Role of Monetary Policy in an Overlapping Generations Model," Cowles Foundation Discussion Paper #656R, Yale University, 1985.
**[24] Debreu, G., *The Theory of Value,* New Haven: Yale University Press, 1959.
**[25] Dornbusch, R. and M. H. Simonsen: *Inflation, Debt, and Indexation.* Cambridge, Mass., MIT Press, 1983.
*[26] Eden, B., "Labor Contracts, Enforcement and Fluctuations in Aggregate Employment: The Case of No Severance Payments," University of Iowa Working Paper, 1983 (revised 1985).
*[27] Farmer, R. E., "A New Theory of Aggregate Supply," *American Economic Review,* **74** (1984), 920–930.
*[28] Farmer, R. E., "Implicit Contracts with Asymmetric Information and Bankruptcy: The Effect of Interest Rates on Layoffs," *Review of Economic Studies,* **52** (1985), 427–442.
[29] Feldstein, M., "Temporary Layoffs in the Theory of Unemployment," *Journal of Political Economy,* **84 (1976), 937–957.
[30] Fethke, G., "The Conformity of Wage-Indexation Models with 'Stylized Facts'," *American Economic Review,* **74** (1985), 856–861.
[31] Fethke, G. and A. Policano, "Wage Contingencies, The Pattern of Negotiation and Aggregate Implications of Alternative Contract Structures," *Journal of Monetary Economics,* **14 (1984), 151–170.
*[32] Fischer, S., "Long-term Contracts, Rational Expectations and the Optimal Money Supply Rule," *Journal of Political Economy,* **85** (1977), 191–205.
**[33] Fischer, S., "Wage Indexation and Macroeconomc Stability", in *Stabilization of the Domestic and International Economy* ed. by K. Brunner and A. Meltzer, New York: North Holland, 1977.
[34] Foster, J. and H. Wu, "Involuntary Unemployment as a Principal-Agent Equilibrium," *American Economic Review,* **74 (1984), 476–484.
**[35] Geanakoplos, J. and T. Ito, "On Implicit Contracts and Involuntary Unemployment," Cowles Foundation Discussion Paper #640, Yale University, 1982.
[36] Geary, P. and J. Kennan, "The Employment-Real Wage Relationship: An International Study," *Journal of Political Economy,* **90 (1982), 854–871.
[37] Gertler, M., "Imperfect Information and Wage Inertia in the Business Cycle," *Journal of Political Economy,* **90 (1982), 967–987.
[38] Gordon, D. F., "A Neo-Classical Theory of Keynesian Unemployment," *Economic Inquiry,* **12 (1974), 431–459.
[39] Gordon, R. J., "Why U.S. Wage and Employment Behavior Differs From That in Britain and Japan," *Economic Journal,* **92 (1982), 13–44.
*[40] Gray, J., "Wage Indexation: A Macroeconomic Approach," *Journal of Monetary Economics,* **2** (1976), 221–235.
*[41] Gray, J., "On Indexation and Contract Length," *Journal of Political Economy,* **86** (1978), 1–18.
*[42] Green, J. and C. Kahn, "Wage Employment Contracts," *Quarterly Journal of Economics* (Supplement), **98** (1983), 173–188.
[43] Grossman, H., "Risk Shifting, Layoffs and Seniority," *Journal of Monetary Economics,* **4 (1978), 661–686.
*[44] Grossman, S. and O. Hart, "Implicit Contracts, Moral Hazard and Unemployment," *American Economic Review* (Paper and Proceedings), **71** (1981), 301–308.

*[45] Grossman, S., "Implicit Contracts Under Asymmetric Information." *Quarterly Journal of Economics* (Supplement), **71** (1983), 123–157.
*[46] Grossman, S., Hart, O. and E. Maskin, "Unemployment with Observable Aggregate Shocks," *Journal of Political Economy,* **91** (1983), 907–928.
*[47] Hall, R., "Employment Fluctuations and Wage Rigidity," *Brookings Papers on Economic Activity,* **1** (1980), 91–123.
*[48] Hall, R. and D. Lilien, "Efficient Wage Bargains Under Uncertain Supply and Demand," *American Eonomic Review,* **69** (1979), 868–879.
[49] Hall, R. and E. Lazear, "The Excess Sensitivity of Layoffs and Quits to Demand," *Journal of Labor Economics,* **2 (1984), 233–258.
[50] Harris, M. and B. Holmstrom, "A Theory of Wage Dynamics," *Review of Economic Studies,* **49** (1982), 315–334.
[51] Harris, M. and A. Raviv, "Some Results on Incentive Contracts," *American Economic Review,* **68 (1978), 20–30.
*[52] Harris, M. and R. Townsend, "Resource Allocation Under Asymmetric Information," *Econometrica,* **49** (1982), 33–64.
*[53] Hart, O., "Optimal Labour Contracts Under Asymmetric Information: An Introduction," *Review of Economic Studies,* **50** (1983), 3–35.
*[54] Hart, O. and B. Holmstrom, "The Theory of Contracts," Massachusetts Institute of Technology Working Paper #418, 1986.
**[55] Hart, O. and J. Moore, "Incomplete Contracts and Renegotiation," London School of Economics, Working Paper, 1985.
*[56] Holmstrom, B., "Moral Hazard and Observability," *The Bell Journal of Economics,* **10** (1979), 74–91.
*[57] Holmstrom, B., "Contractual Models of the Labor Market," *American Economics Review,* **71** (1981), 308–313.
*[58] Holmstrom, B., "Equilibrium Long-term Contracts," *Quarterly Journal of Economics* (Supplement), **98** (1983), 23–54.
*[59] Hosios, A., "Layoffs, Recruitment and Interfirm Mobility," *Journal of Labor Economics,* forthcoming, 1986.
[60] Ioannides, Y. and C. Pissarides, "Wages and Employment with Firm Specific Seniority," *The Bell Journal of Economics,* **14 (1983), 573–581.
[61] Ito, T., "Labour Contracts with Voluntary Quits," Working Paper, University of Minnesota, 1984.
*[62] Kahn, C., "Optimal Severance Pay with Incomplete Information," *Journal of Political Economy,* **93** (1985), 435–451.
[63] Kahn, C. and J. Scheinkman, "Optimal Employment Contracts with Bankruptcy Constraints," *Journal of Economic Theory,* **35 (1985), 343–365.
**[64] Kamien, M. and N. Schwartz, *Dynamic Optimization: The Calculus of Variations and Optimal Control in Economics and Management.* New York: North-Holland, 1981.
[65] Kihlstrom, R. and J. J. Laffont, "A General Equilibrium Entrepreneurial Theory of Firm Formation Based on Risk Aversion," *Journal of Political Economy,* 87 (1979), 719–748.
[66] Klein, B. and K. Leffler, "The Role of Market Forces in Assuring Contractual Performance," *Journal of Political Economy,* **89 (1981), 615–641.
[67] Litterman, R. and L. Weiss, "Money, Real Interest Rates, and Output: a Reinterpretation of Postwar U.S. Data," *Econometrica,* **53 (1985), 129–156.
*[68] Lucas, R. E., "Expectations and the Neutrality of Money," *Journal of Economic Theory,* **4** (1972), 103–124.

[69] Lucas, R. E., "Some International Evidence on Output-Inflation Tradeoffs," *American Economic Review,* **63 (1973), 326–334.

[70] McCallum, B., "Rational Expectations and Macroeconomic Stabilization Policy," *Journal of Money, Credit and Banking,* **12** (1980), 716–746.

[71] McDonald, I. and R. Solow, "Wage Bargaining and Employment," *American Economic Review,* **71** (1981) 896–908.

*[72] Moore, J., "Optimal Labour Contracts When Workers have a Variety of Privately Observed Reservation Wages," *Review of Economic Studies,* **52** (1985), 37–67.

*[73] Moore, J., "Contracting Between Two Parties With Private Information," London School of Economics Working Paper, 1984.

*[74] Mortenson, D., "A Welfare Analysis of Unemployment Insurance: Variation on Second Best Themes," *Carnegie-Rochester Series on Public Policy,* **19** (1983), 67–98.

*[75] Myerson, R., "Incentive Compatibility and the Bargaining Problem," *Econometrica,* **47** (1979), 61–74.

*[76] Phelps, E. and J. Taylor, "Stabilizing Powers of Monetary Policy Under Rational Expectation," *Journal of Political Economy,* **85** (1977), 163–190.

[77] Polemarchakis, H., "Implicit Contracts and Employment Theory," *Review of Economic Studies,* **46** (1979), 97–108.

[78] Polemarchakis, H. and L. Weiss, "Fixed Wages, Layoffs, Unemployment Compensation and Welfare," *American Economic Review,* **68** (1978), 909–917.

[79] Prescott, E., "Can the Cycle be Reconciled with a Consistent Theory of Expectations or a Progress Report on Business Cycle Theory," Federal Reserve Bank of Minneapolis, Working Paper #239, 1983.

[80] Riddell, W. C., "The Empirical Foundations of the Phillips Curve: Evidence from Canadian Wage Contract Data," *Econometrica,* **37** (1979), 1–24.

* [81] Riordan, M., "Uncertainty, Asymmetric Information and Bilateral Contracts," *Review of Economic Studies,* **51** (1984), 83–93.

*[82] Rosen, S., "Implicit Contracts, A Survey," *Journal of Economic Literature,* **23** (1985), 1144–1175.

[83] Sachs, J., "Wages, Profits and Macroeconomic Adjustment: A Comparative Study," *Brookings Papers on Econimic Activity,* **2 (1979), 269–319.

*[84] Sappington, D., "Limited Liability Contracts Between Principal and Agent," *Journal of Economic Theory,* **29** (1983), 1–21.

[85] Sargent, T., *Macroeconomic Theory.* New York: Academic Press, 1979.

*[86] Sargent, T. and N. Wallace: "Rational Expectations, the Optimal Monetary Instruments and the Optimal Money Supply," *Journal of Political Economy,* **83** (1975), 241–254.

[87] Shapiro, C., "Consumer Information, Product Quality and Seller Reputation," *The Bell Journal of Economics,* **13 (1982), 20–35.

*[88] Shapiro, C. and J. Stiglitz, "Equilibrium Unemployment as a Worker Incentive Device," *American Economic Review,* **74** (1984), 433–444.

[89] Smith, B., "A Model of Nominal Contract," Federal Reserve Bank of Minneapolis, Working Paper #260, 1984.

*[90] Stiglitz, J., "Theories of Wage Rigidity," in *Keynes Economic Legacy: Contemporary Economic Theories* ed. by James Butkiewicz, Kenneth Koford and Jeffrey Miller, New York: Praeger Publishers, 1986, 153–206.

*[91] Taylor, J., "Aggregate Dynamics and Staggered Contracts," *Journal of Political Economy,* **88** (1980), 1–23.

[92] Taylor, J., "Union Wage Settlements During a Disinflation," *American Economic Review,* **73** (1983), 981–993.

*[93] Weitzman, M., "Some Macroeconomic Implications of Alternative Compensation Schemes," *Economic Journal,* **93** (1983), 763–783.
*[94] Williamson, O., "Transaction-Cost Economics: The Governance of Contractual Relations," *Journal of Law and Economics,* **22** (1979), 233–261.
**[95] Wright, R., "Labor Markets and Labor Contracts in a Dynamic General Equilibrium Model," Cornell University, 1985.
[96] Yellen, J., "Efficiency Wage Models of Unemployment," *American Economic Review,* **74 (1984), 200–205.

Appendix A: Proof of Proposition 2

Proof Using Proposition 1, the optimal contract is characterized by an hours schedule and a wage schedule. For simplicity, consider a contract specifying an hour's schedule, $h(s)$, and a *compensation* schedule, $c(s)$. The hourly wage is then $c(s)/h(s)$.

With this notation and Proposition 1, (1) and (2) become

$$sf'(Nh)G(c, h) = 0,$$

and

$$\lambda U_c^e(c, h) - NV'(\pi(s)) = 0.$$

Total differentiation of these equations and application of Kramer's rule implies that

$$\frac{dh}{ds} = \frac{-f'(\lambda U_{cc}^e + V''N) + G_c V'' f N}{K}.$$

Here $K > 0$ by the second-order conditions for the contracting problem. So $dh/ds > 0$ as long as the numerator is positive.

Letting $A^w \equiv {}^-U_{cc}/U_c$ and $A^F \equiv -V''/V'$ measure the income curvatures of the preferences for workers and the firm respectively and using the first-order conditions,

$$\frac{dh}{ds} = V'\left[A_w + A_F\left(1 - \frac{G_c f}{f'}\right)\right].$$

In this expression G_c is the partial derivative of a workers' marginal rate of substitution with respect to c. By direct calculation,

$$G_c = \frac{1}{U_c}\left(\frac{U_{cc}U_h}{U_c} - U_{ch}\right).$$

Assuming that leisure is a normal good is equivalent to assuming $G_c > 0$. Hence, the sign of dh/ds is ambiguous if leisure is a normal good.

If firms are close to being risk neutral and workers are risk averse, then dh/ds is clearly positive. Otherwise, the sign of dh/ds depends on A^w, A^F and G_c.

Appendix B

The purpose of this appendix is to provide a formal proof of Proposition 3. The approach taken in the proof, which is only a slight modification of that found in Green–Kahn [42], can be useful in other contexts, such as the case of worker asymmetric information studied in Section 3.

To start, we consider the specification of the truthtelling constraints for the firm. As $\tilde{s}$ is a continuous random variable taking values in the interval $[\underline{s}, \bar{s}]$, we can replace (22) with the first and second order conditions to the ex post problem of maximize $sf(h(m)) - w(m)$. See the discussion in Green–Kahn [42] and Kahn–Scheinkman [63] on this procedure. Truthtelling requires that the announced state (m) equals the true state (s) for all s or that

$$sf'(h(s))\dot{h}(s) - \dot{w}(s) = 0 \tag{B1}$$

and

$$sf''(h(s))\dot{h}(s) + sf'(h(s))\frac{d\dot{h}(s)}{ds} - \frac{d\dot{w}(s)}{ds} \leq 0 \tag{B2}$$

for all s where $\dot{h}(s) \equiv dh/ds$ and $\dot{w}(s) \equiv dw/ds$.

Here equations (B1) is the first-order condition for the firm's choice problem over m and (B2) is the second-order condition evaluated at $m = s$. Since (B1) holds for all s, we can totally differentiate (B1) to obtain

$$f'(h(s))\dot{h}(s) + sf''(h(s))\dot{h}(s) + sf'(h(s))\frac{d\dot{h}(s)}{ds} - \frac{d\dot{w}(s)}{ds} = 0 \quad \text{for all } s. \tag{B3}$$

Together, (B2) and (B3) imply that the necessary and sufficient conditions for implementation are (B1) and $\dot{h}(s) \geq 0$. So, the optimization problem for an optimal contract $\delta \equiv \{w(s), h(s)\}$ is then

$$\underset{\delta}{\text{maximize}}\, E_s\{sf(h(s)) - w(s)\}$$

subject to $E_s U(w(s), h(s)) \geq \bar{U}$

$$\dot{h}(s) \geq 0$$

and (B1).

Let $p(s)$ be the probability that state s occurs and let λ be the multiplier in the expected utility constraint for the worker. We analyze this problem using optimal control methods (see Kamien–Schwartz [64]). We view $k \equiv \dot{h}$ as the control variable so that the Hamiltonian associated with this problem is

$$H \equiv p(s)[sf(h(s)) - w(s) + \lambda U(w(s), h(s))] + \phi(s)ksf'(h(s)) + \eta(s)k$$

where $\phi(s)$ and $\eta(s)$ are co-state variables. The conditions describing the optimal contract are

$$\phi(s)sf'(h(s)) = -\eta(s), \tag{B4}$$

$$\phi(s) = p(s)(1 - \lambda U_w(w(s), h(s)), \tag{B5}$$

and

$$- \dot{\eta}(s) = p(s)(sf'(h(s)h + \lambda U_h(w(s), h(s))$$
$$+ k\phi(s)sf''(h(s)) \quad \text{for all } s. \tag{B6}$$

Total differentiation of (B4) and substitutions into (B5) and (B6) yield

$$sf'(h(s)) = \frac{\phi f'(h(s)}{p(s)\lambda U_w(\cdot)} - \frac{U_h(\cdot)}{U_w(\cdot)}. \tag{B7}$$

Hence the form of the employment distortion depends on a sign of $\phi(s)$. If $\phi(s) > 0$, then $sf'(h(s)) > -U_h(\cdot)/U_w(\cdot)$ so that underemployment arises. If $\phi(s) < 0$, then overemployment arises.

Totally differentiating (B5) and substituting (B7) yields

$$\dot{\phi}(s) = p'(s)(1 - \lambda U_w) - p(s)\lambda k\left[\frac{U_{ww}\phi f'}{p\lambda U_w} - \frac{U_{ww}U_h}{U_w} + U_{wh}\right]. \tag{B8}$$

As discussed in [64], $\phi(s)$ is continuous and differentiable. The transversality conditions for this problem (see Green–Kahn [42]) are $\phi(\underline{s}) = \phi(\bar{s}) = 0$. We now use these properties and conditions to prove Proposition 3.

Proof of Proposition 3 With $\phi(\underline{s}) = \phi(\bar{s}) = 0$, then there exists $\hat{s}$ such that $\dot{\phi}(\hat{s}) = 0$ where $\hat{s} \in [\underline{s}, \bar{s}]$. Using (B5), at $s = \hat{s}$, (B8) is therefore

$$\ddot{\phi}(\hat{s}) = -p(\hat{s})\lambda k\left[\frac{U_{ww}\phi f'}{p\lambda U_w} - \frac{U_{ww}U_h}{U_w} + U_{wh}\right]. \tag{B9}$$

When leisure is a normal good, $\lambda > 0$, $k > 0$ and $p(s) > 0$, (B9) implies that if $\phi(\hat{s}) > 0$, then $\ddot{\phi}(\hat{s}) > 0$ too. However, this is inconsistent with the transversality conditions and the continuity of $\phi(s)$ which together imply that if $\phi(\hat{s}) > 0$, then $\ddot{\phi}(\hat{s}) < 0$ for any $\hat{s}$ such that $\dot{\phi}(\hat{s}) = 0$. Hence, if leisure is normal $\phi(s) \leq 0$. Note that unless worker preferences satisfy (24), $\phi(s)$ must be strictly negative as the first-best allocation is not implementable. Therefore when leisure is a normal good, $\phi(s) < 0$ for $s \in (\underline{s}, \bar{s})$ and hence overemployment arises. When leisure is an inferior good, $\phi(s) > 0$ for $s \in (\underline{s}, \bar{s})$ can be shown in a similar way and underemployment arises. QED.

It should be noted that this proof used the condition of complete separation across states: i.e., $k(s) > 0$ for all s. See Kahn–Scheinkman [63] and the references therein for a discussion of pooling and related issues.

INDEX